A PRAYER BOOK FOR WRITERS

COURTNEY KLEEFELD

A PRAYER BOOK FOR WRITERS

Copyright © 2020 by Courtney Kleefeld

All rights reserved. This book or any portion thereof may not be reproduced or used in any manner whatsoever without the express written permission of the publisher except for the use of brief quotations in a book review.

Scripture quotations marked (NLT) are taken from the Holy Bible, New Living Translation, copyright ©1996, 2004, 2015 by Tyndale House Foundation. Used by permission of Tyndale House Publishers, a Division of Tyndale House Ministries, Carol Stream, Illinois 60188. All rights reserved.

ISBN: 9798619955019

Design by Lisa Kleefeld

To anyone who aches for connection with God,
and to anyone who seeks Him;
Don't. Give. Up.

TABLE OF CONTENTS

Introduction ix

PART I: WRITING

Creativity • 5
Ideas • 17
God's Voice • 21
Decisions • 25
Routine • 33
Fiction • 39
Nonfiction • 51
Characters • 55
Outlining • 61
Insecurities • 69
Stuck • 75
Writing the First Draft • 87
Rewriting • 109
Revision & Editing • 113
The Final Edits • 117

PART II: PUBLISHING

The Decision • 125
Preparation • 129
Traditional • 137
Self-Publishing • 141
Fears • 147
Finding Support • 151
Marketing • 155

PART III: LIFE

God • 163
Holy Spirit • 193
Worship • 201
Health • 207
Relationships • 223
Work & Stewardship • 243

PART IV: PRAYING FOR OTHER WRITERS

Notes • 273

Don't worry about anything; instead, pray about everything. Tell God what you need and thank him for all he has done. Then you will experience God's peace, which exceeds anything we can understand. His peace will guard your hearts and minds as you live in Christ Jesus.

Philippians 4:6-7, NLT

INTRODUCTION

WHY A PRAYER BOOK FOR WRITERS?

I partially wrote this book for myself, with a lot of prayer over it, so that I could use it throughout my life as a writer and build off of it. I also wrote it thinking of various online Christian writing communities because I had seen many believers voicing a difficulty both in drawing close to God and in understanding whether or not their writing glorified God — I too struggled with this, and I still struggle with questions about what makes an excellent book in God's eyes, not just in the dominant opinion of current evangelical church-goers. I think we often struggle with this question because of the way many skeptical Christians, having heard that we are writers, have asked us, "Does your writing glorify God?"

My question in reply would be this: How can we know?

It is an important question to me, as a Christian, because I want every area of my life to be influenced by the gospel. So I will continue to seek out the answer with its many layers, even as I discover clues.

Writing is a very spiritual aspect of my life because stories were what originally gave me the desire to seek God with everything in my power. Fairy tales, great fantasy stories, and classics, they all helped me understand certain concepts in the Bible, such as the importance of developing and keeping a child-like wonder. They gave me examples of what Christ-like sacrifice looked like. I believe those stories glorify God in some way.

Many great stories were not written by Christians. The stories are good because of their power, vulnerability, and humility.

I believe that if we want to write great stories, it will behoove us to seek truth, to draw close to God, and to embark on a quest to be honest with ourselves and with God about everything; what is in our souls usually comes out in our writing, whether we want it to or not.

The most powerful testimonies are often striking because of the vulnerability and courage of their speakers. So too are the most powerful stories so often striking because of the vulnerability and courage of their writers.

One of the challenges that came when writing this book was the need for me to re-examine my own prayer habits and to acknowledge the state of my heart. Throughout the writing process of this book, both in drafting and in rounds of edits, these prayers have reminded me to align myself to connect with God by acknowledging His goodness and remembering the good things He has done in my life. Remembering the good helps me have faith, even when thinking about the good doesn't always make me feel better.

The prayers have reminded me to reaffirm my faith in the midst of doubt. Lastly, they have reminded me to continue to rediscover God's unconditional, magnificent love. I know I am not alone in struggling with sin, anxiety, or the common writing struggles of insecurity and procrastination. I want to share these prayers with you in hope that they will draw you closer to God, both as a creative writer and as a whole human being, loved by God.

One might ask, "why pray over every aspect of the writing process? Isn't that like asking God to micro-manage your writing? Wouldn't that take away creativity?"

It's not so much asking God to give me commands over every aspect of a book so that I don't have to make any creative decisions — I believe God gave us the ability to be creative for a reason, and He wants us to use the creativity He has given us. Having said that, I believe God wants to be invited into the writing process of our books. He has something to say to us about our stories. He knows how to make them even better than we ever could on our own.

When I pray over my writing, I notice I become more creative, not less, and praying helps me fight against the fears that try to keep me from writing.

Many of us have books inside of us, whether or not we feel specifically that God wants us to write them, but we struggle with fears: fear that we can't write well, fear that no one will like our writing, fear that we won't be able to financially support ourselves either way, fear of failing or of succeeding, fear that it is somehow not God's will for us to write, fear that we won't write something that glorifies God.

Writing is often an act of spiritual warfare, and our enemy the devil does not want us to write anything that would bring profound truth, light, and beauty into the world, and certainly not anything effective in the world of literature. But we don't have to be afraid of him because Jesus already defeated him, God has angels protecting us, and the powerful Holy Spirit lives inside of us, ready to equip us for any spiritual warfare we may encounter when writing a significantly spiritual book God has called us to write.

Building ourselves up in biblical truth and remaining anchored in Christ are our greatest challenges as believers.

Praying about everything, including writing, helps me begin to let go of the worries I am able to let go of, and it helps me write even when I'm afraid.

HOW TO USE THIS BOOK

You are welcome to use these prayers as much as you need. If a prayer does not express what you think or feel, I pray that it draws up the words that have been buried down deep inside of you, the words you need to pray the most in that moment. Write down your prayers in a journal to keep track of them, pray aloud, or pray silently.

If you are preparing to write a book, whether for the first time or for the twentieth time, the first chapter of prayers on creativity may help you prepare your heart for the creative process. If, on the other hand, you are looking firstly for prayers for your personal life and relationship with God, you can go straight to Part III of the book and read from that section first.

Underneath some of the prayers are Scripture references to look up if you want to read them as a supplemental devotional. A few blank, lined pages have been provided at the end of the book for your use.

I won't say these are "the correct" prayers to pray for each person, because everyone has different needs, and everyone will experience a different prayer on page one.

Furthermore, my college major is in writing, not theology. I have only read one or two books about prayer in my lifetime this far, outside of the books of the Bible. What I write here is pulled from many years of experience of my own relationship with God, with its ups and downs.

Prayer is a conversation, an attempt to connect with God. It is a way to process one's feelings before Him and come into His presence, just like how talking through things with a friend and feeling their reassurance helps. Praying aloud, even if it's just in a whisper, helps center me and focus my attention on Him.

Prayer is also a way for me to begin to surrender myself and my desires to God so He can purify them, helping me see the good and the bad.

I can't improve myself through my efforts alone, so I go to God; He is the one who transforms me, and then I can't boast. This is a part of the Christian life in relationship with God.

Sometimes, when I don't know what else to pray, I pray The Lord's Prayer from Matthew 6:9-13, or I go to Psalms and read some of the prayers that David prayed. These are foundational places in the Bible, and so much truth can be found in them.

For a little bit of background, I'm a nondenominational Christian believer who adheres to the Apostle's Creed and believes in the active gifts of the Holy Spirit. I believe God guides His people today in many different ways, the first one being through revelation of the truths in His Word.

HOW THIS BOOK IS DIVIDED

The book is divided into four main parts:

- Part I: Writing
- Part II: Publishing
- Part III: Life
- Part IV: Praying for Other Writers

Part I contains chapters of prayers about the writing process — preparing oneself to write, brainstorming ideas, choosing a genre, outlining, writing the first draft, getting unstuck, letting the first draft sit, rewriting the book, and editing the final draft.

Within this part is also a section of prayers for specific genres within fiction and nonfiction. When you have an idea of what genre or type of story you are thinking of writing — adventure, fantasy, contemporary, science fiction, etcetera, or memoir, theology, or other nonfiction genre — you might look at these prayers and find one for that genre.

Part II contains chapters of prayers about the publishing process — the decision of whether to publish, the decision of whether to go with traditional publishing or self-publishing, finding an agent, the publishing process, working with a book cover designer, working with an editor, finding support, and marketing the book.

Part III contains chapters of prayers about life — Your relationship with God, your relationship with yourself, your relationships with others, personal responsibilities, vocation, and money. This section is very important for any writer because your life outside writing will often influence how much time you spend writing, how much energy you have to write, what you write, and how much time you can spend educating yourself on how to write better.

There is a small chapter of prayers about the fruits and gifts of the Holy Spirit later in this part; you don't have to use them if you don't believe in the gifts, but if you are interested, scripture references that help explain the gifts of the Holy Spirit have been provided at the bottom of those prayers.

Part IV is a small collection of prayers for other writers — a prayer for your favorite living author, prayers for your friends who write, prayers for other Christian writers, and prayers for the writing community.

A few prayers scattered throughout the book mention counseling and mental health. Those prayers are especially for people who struggle with anxiety or depression, though anyone can benefit from constructive counseling, and everyone struggles with worry at some point in life.

I have struggled with general anxiety disorder for many years before beginning to discover various health problems that had at least partially caused the anxiety. With God's help, I began to find ways to improve my health, though it has been hard.

WHAT THIS BOOK MEANS TO ME

The week after a significant turning point in my life in late Spring of 2018, I desperately wanted a project to work on, something to do with my hands, something to get my mind off of the shame and shock that I felt over what had happened.

I began to pray, and I asked others to pray with me for wisdom of what to write. The idea for this book came, or rather, returned to me, just a few days later. It was an idea I had thought about a few months before but had forgotten about it. The idea suddenly felt fresh and exciting to me, so I began working on it immediately.

This project was an indirect way for me to begin deep healing, and soon I began imagining how it might be divided up and organized.

As if in confirmation that God was calling me to write this book, I finished the rough draft in one month — faster than I'd finished any other book draft. Everything flowed so smoothly. After this, I asked several peers in my writing community for feedback, sent out digital copies of the draft, and waited. About a month later, feedback started coming in. Here is where I started working on re-writing and editing the book. An editor friend was willing to do a few rounds of edits. Later, my sister also sent me many suggestions for changes. Over the course of writing and editing this book, several people have either prayed over this book with me or have spoken good words over it.

The rewriting and editing process was tricky. As I considered each prayer, I asked myself the following questions:

When you wrote this prayer, were you being completely honest with yourself and with God about what you thought, felt, and wanted?

Were you acknowledging God's goodness, power, knowledge, love, grace, mercy, tenderness, patience, and sovereignty?

These were questions that I realized I also had to bring to God in prayer by myself, because in some instances, I couldn't tell what I really thought and felt. This revelation made me realize that I needed to find out what I really thought and felt. It also made me realize that I needed to find out how to be honest with myself and with God about everything.

God wants us to be honest with Him. He is never shocked by our questions or our struggles; rather, He invites us to come to Him with them, so He can walk with us through them. One of my biggest challenges in writing this book was to make sure I was portraying these struggles accurately and not belittling or overlooking them. Many of these struggles are common to humanity, and especially creatives.

The quest for complete and total honesty, both about ourselves and about God, is important if we want to be close to God in relationship.

Acknowledging who God truly is helps us connect with and experience His love.

I pray that you find comfort in the pages of this book, as well as the ability to draw closer to God than you ever imagined. He longs for you to experience His love personally, both in your daily life and in your creative process. God is the great creator, and we are made in His image. Coming close to Him is a journey, with ups and downs. I encourage you to embrace this journey.

May God bless and keep you.

PART I
WRITING

DEAR GOD,

Please help me write something today.

In Jesus' name,
Amen.

CREATIVITY

A NEW JOURNEY

Dear God,

I want to create something beautiful. I want to experience it and then share it with people in ways they will be able to understand, ponder, imagine, and feel. Take me on a journey to know You better in this process. Give me the patience I need to write a work and the patience to take care of myself in the process.

Awaken in me a sense of curiosity. Teach me to ask questions — questions to myself about the books I'm writing, but also about ideas and the art of writing itself. Bring to my attention what I should focus on during this creative journey; inspire within me the questions that will lead me closer to You, for You are the source and embodiment of Love, Truth, Beauty, and Wonder.

Let Your will be done in me as it is in heaven.

In Jesus' name,
Amen.

Genesis 1

THE LOVE OF GOD

Dear God,

I have heard about you all my life, and I am a Christian, but the story of the gospel has lost its emotional power for me. I want to know you and be close to your heart, not only to know things about you. I have heard of your love, but I want to experience it. I want this relationship with you to become real to me so that it influences every area of my life. I want to follow you.

What do you think of me? What do you feel towards me? I'm just one person out of so many humans who have lived. How could you care about me specifically?

Help me develop a passion for you; help me seek you with perseverance. Help me find you.

In Jesus' name,
Amen.

Zephaniah 3:17

SIGNIFICANCE OF CREATIVITY

Dear God,

Help me know that you care about me, that you care about my writing, that you care about stories and creativity. I know it in my head, but it's hard to really believe. Can I worship you by writing stories? Are stories valuable to you?

Lead me to books that excite you, books you know I would like — books that would inspire me and give me ideas for the story you have entrusted to me to write.

Help me see another side of you that I don't know yet, Lord. Let me feel your excitement about writing. Do you get inspired?

Let me come to know and believe deep down that you want me to talk to you about anything and everything on my mind, anytime and anywhere. Help me see that you delight in me.

In Jesus' name,
Amen

John 1

COURAGE TO WRITE

Dear God,

Please give me a courage so firmly rooted in You that nothing can stop it. Courage to write the type of story that I love, even if I don't know many other people who like the genre. Courage to tell the truth.

Courage to begin.

Give me enough courage for today. Help me bring glory to You in how I write and think and in how I treat everyone. Thank You for the courage You have given me in past situations. Thank You for hearing me and guiding me in this season.

In Jesus' name,
Amen.

EXCELLENCE

Dear God,

Help me understand what excellence means to You when it comes to writing. Help me care the right amount about writing excellently and know what I should do. Show me how to understand and gracefully acknowledge my strengths and weaknesses as a writer. Let me realize the importance of different elements of excellence. Show me what steps I should take to write stronger books.

In Jesus' name,
Amen.

BECOMING LIKE A CHILD

Dear God,

You desire that I become like a child. Help me understand what this means for me and where I am. I feel as though, through the years, I have lost something crucial to living. Something I once had as a child. Help me regain a childlike innocence in the ways that You desire while continuing to mature and learn how to follow better in Your ways. Lead me by the hand in this process to rediscover the beauty of faith in You and in the principles of Your Kingdom. Awaken a habit of wonder inside of me so I can remember how small I am and how big You are.

In my daily life, help me notice details I didn't notice before. Remind me to take some time to savor them in silence. Maybe I'll write a poem to help me notice both the ordinary and extraordinary around me.

In Jesus' name,
Amen.

Matthew 19:13-14

A DAY TO PLAY WITH PROSE

Dear God,

Today, I'm going to practice playing with prose. Thank You, Lord, for the ability to play with words and see what happens when they are put in different combinations for fun. There's a lot I can do with words, I'm sure, and I'm excited to see where this takes me, doing it with You. Today, I don't care about getting the words right. I'm just experimenting and having fun and hearing You laugh with me over the words I'm going to play with. Teach me, Lord, to continue learning not to be so serious that I can't laugh at my writing or laugh at myself in good humor. Teach me the art of play.

In Jesus' name,
Amen.

TAKING RISKS

Dear God,

Give me wisdom about when to take creative risks. Help me learn how to play with these ideas. Help me be willing to try something new. I want to do something different than what everyone else has already done. I don't want any fear to cripple my creativity, either, Lord. I want to master this craft and confidently take risks that will allow me to grow as a writer and grow closer to You. You, Lord, know the cost of such risks. Help me be willing to fail at whatever it is I'm trying to write well, if only to learn from the experience and gain new revelation of what may work. Teach me how to see my writing life as an adventure, Lord, and help me accept each part of it with mercy. Shape me as You will.

In Jesus' name,
Amen.

A DAY TO PRACTICE

Dear God,

Today, I'm going to practice writing something small — a short story, a writing prompt — so I can create something without pressure and gain experience while learning how to play. Thank You, Lord, for this gift. Work in me and lead me to fascinating discoveries. Shape me as I learn how to play.

In Jesus' name,
Amen.

WHAT KIND OF WRITER

Dear God,

Show me what kind of writer I can be, what kind of writing I can do, and how I can go about it. Give me wisdom about where my boundaries could be when it comes to how dark a project is or what kind of content will go into it, if I need that type of boundary. Help me give myself healthy rules that will help me have an attuned focus. I don't want to try to write something that will cause me or others more harm than good. Give me wisdom about how to keep myself mentally healthy through all of my projects during and outside the writing process. Help me take responsibility for the wisdom You bring to my attention; help me apply wisdom to my life effectively, Lord. Let Your wonderful will be done on earth as it is in heaven. Please, do not let the struggles in my life stop me from doing what You have invited me to do.

In Jesus' name,
Amen.

Galatians 5:25

OUT OF THE INNERMOST

Dear God,

Please help me write a book out of the innermost part of my soul — not half-heartedly and timidly, but full-heartedly and courageously, with authenticity and skill.

Help me forget about trying to please everyone. Help me turn off the inner critic as I write.

Help me take my writing seriously, even when my inner critic mocks it.

Show me how to write a book that is bigger on the inside.

Let Your beautiful will be done in my life as it is in heaven.

In Jesus' name,
Amen.

IDEAS

WHAT TO WRITE

Dear God,

Today, I want to look for some ideas for a project to write; I have a notebook and pen so I can collect them on paper. Help me find a good idea that I like. It doesn't have to be a huge one. I want to finish something and learn from the experience.

In Jesus' name,
Amen.

AN IDEA

Dear God,

I got excited about this one idea that I've written down. Thank You for helping me find it.

In Jesus' name,
Amen.

DEVELOPING THE IDEA

Dear God,

As I develop this idea, help me find the amount of complexity for the project that works best for me as a writer. Let me make this book not so complex that I can't write it, nor so simple that I don't want to write it anymore.

Help me find where my ideas fit together regarding this project; help me appreciate the end result.

In Jesus' name,
Amen.

GOD'S VOICE

PRAYER TO HEAR GOD'S VOICE

Dear God,

Please open my ears to hear Your voice. Help me recognize when You are speaking to me. I want to be open to what You have to say to me.

Thank You for Your Word, which has wisdom and divine power within its pages. Guide me to specific places in the Bible that will help me on my journey, Yahweh; let Your truths sink deep into my heart and create a strong foundation there that will make me a stronger person and a more confident writer.

Help me recognize the ways that You speak to me, Lord, and keep me from making up Your voice, too.

Protect me from the devil and from his lies in every facet of my life, including writing. Help me identify unhealthy, obsessive or intrusive thoughts whenever they come, and help me find the root of them with the guidance of a counselor if needed. Help me find healing and freedom from obsessive thoughts and lies so that I can write with a clear mind.

Help me have faith that in wanting a relationship with me, You also want me to hear and know Your voice and obey it, even if I never hear Your voice audibly or through my thoughts. I will sense Your loving guidance and choose to expect it in the future writing process and in other areas of my life.

Thank You, Lord, for the Holy Spirit, who brings peace and confirmation that I belong to You because I believe in Your son's death and resurrection, and because I rely on Jesus' sacrifice for salvation. Let confidence grow within me, for I am one of Your beloved children. You are my shepherd. Let Your perfect will be done in my life.

In Jesus' name,
Amen.

John 10, James 1

LISTENING

Dear God,

Remind me to spend time listening to You, believing that You will speak to me. That second part is hard. It's often easier for me to pray and then move on with my day or go to sleep than to really stop, listen, and believe that You have something to say to me, or that I will be able to hear or sense it. I know You are good. I also don't want to open up my mind to deception. Give me wisdom about that. And I don't want to sound off my own ideas and pretend that they are from You, but my mind never turns off, God. It's hard to tell if it's You talking or me talking sometimes. I know the importance of reading Your Word and gleaning truth from it, but I also know that sometimes the Holy Spirit has a specific word for me in my life, whether it be direction or wisdom. Help me be open to that, God. Teach me how to have faith in this aspect of my relationship with You. Let Your will be done in me, today.

In Jesus' name,
Amen.

Psalm 29

COURAGE TO HEAR

Dear God,

Give me courage to listen. Give me courage to hear Your voice, Lord, no matter what You have to say to me.

Give me courage to be still in Your presence. Give me courage to make this a regular thing, Lord.

In the stillness, help me confront and gradually break apart the lies I believe that keep me from being close to You, Lord. Teach and remind me of Your life-giving truths in ways that connect to me on an emotional level as well as an intellectual level. Shape me into who You want me to be, Lord, and keep me from anything that would cause me to fall away from You. Thank You.

In Jesus' name,
Amen.

Psalm 46

DECISIONS

PUZZLE

Dear God,

I have an abundance of ideas, but I don't know which ones fit in this book and which ones go in another. Please help me discover and recognize the pieces this story needs while setting aside the pieces that will fit better in a future story. Let them still turn out wonderfully even though I have to move them to another project to clear the way for the core elements of this current project.

Give me peace in this process
as I make these decisions.

In Jesus' name,
Amen.

WHAT TO WRITE FIRST

Dear God,

Show me what part of the story could be fun to play with first. Help me know if I am the sort of writer who works well writing the beginning, middle, or end of the book first. If it would be more helpful for me to write the beginning later, lead me to a scene I can easily write first. I open myself up to creative ideas. Help me align myself with the Holy Spirit so that Your inspiration comes to me naturally and directs me to wherever I need to focus.

Guide my focus at the beginning of the writing process for the book, Yahweh. Please, help me work through insecurities about my writing, and give me the motivation and drive that I need to begin this book, keep writing it, and finish strongly in good time. Give me patience with myself and with the story as I begin the first draft. Help me have fun playing with words. Thank You, Lord.

In Jesus' name,
Amen.

OUTLINING VS. PANTSING

Dear God,

Help me find out what kind of outline would best help me or how much planning this book needs. Help me explore and then write, plan some more and then write, or let me focus on finding out the end of the story first and moving backward from there. Let me know my main character's inner struggle and character arc, and help me build the story around it if that's what should be done. Help me become decisive about my writing process and then stick to it and get the rough draft written. Help me find out what works best for me; but also, how would You go about doing this, God? Let Your name be glorified in what happens concerning this. Help me see Your hand working in this area of my writing life. Thank You, Lord, for the gift of writing.

In Jesus' name,
Amen.

MULTIPLE PROJECTS

Dear God,

I have multiple projects that I could work on. Should I work on just one of them till it's finished and then move on to the next one, or am I the kind of writer who can work on multiple projects simultaneously without a problem? Give me wisdom to decide what to do. Help me give my current project the attention and time that it needs.

In Jesus' name,
Amen.

MAKING NEW

Dear God,

I'm looking at the big picture of this story, but I've looked at it for so long that everything about it now seems dull and cliché, even though it might not be. When I sit down to write this story, make it fresh to me, Lord. Inspire me and show me how to see the story in a new way that infuses every page with new life. Help me appreciate this story and find life in its pages, both while writing it and while reading the drafts back to myself. If there are any dull ideas that could be switched out or better developed, lead me in that, Lord. Shape this story and guide my hands like a potter teaching a child how to mold clay. Shape my imagination to see new possibilities and pick out the most beautiful and meaningful ones. Help me write it excellently.

In Jesus' name,
Amen.

WHEN TO DECIDE

Dear God,

I have been changing around this plot for years now. Please, give me wisdom about when to stop brainstorming and start writing the project. It's because I've changed in the last few years, isn't it? I think I'm ready to come to a conclusion about the characters, plot, theme — everything — but I want peace about committing to a particular version. Let this all happen in Your timing. Thank You for being with me all these years. Thank You for being my best friend. Let Your will be done in my writing life as it is in heaven.

In Jesus' name,
Amen.

EXCUSES

Dear God,

I've been procrastinating on this book because I've come up with so many reasons why I "shouldn't" be writing it, but I've realized that the voice telling me these things is not Your voice but the voice of fear. Help me jump into writing, Lord. You want me to write. Being creative is healthy for me. I choose to begin writing with intention to finish something good. My work won't be perfect, and that's okay. Perfection is limited. The book will be real, and I will become a better writer for having written it and learned. Help me do this, Lord. Thank You for everything.

In Jesus' name,
Amen.

Psalm 119:96, Ecclesiastes 5:18-20

DECIDING ON AN OUTLINE

Dear God,

I'm about to choose between the various outlines I've written for this project. If there are any other changes or variations on the outlines I've written down, inspire me to write them. Guide me and give me peace for the one I will ultimately choose. Help me respect my own decisions to a healthy extent instead of second-guessing myself.

I am learning that, sometimes, sticking to a plan is better than trying to find the "perfect" plan. I am willing to serve You with my creativity. Let me learn while writing this book, knowing that with Your help, I will write something worth reading. Thank You, Lord, for hearing me and giving me wisdom.

In Jesus' name,
Amen.

ROUTINE

THE BEST WRITING LIFE

Dear God,

Help me figure out what works best for me when it comes to the writing life. Because it has so many aspects, it can get overwhelming. Help me keep track of which routine practices work most effectively for me and what will be healthiest for me. I will listen to You and expect to sense and recognize Your guidance today. Thank You for loving me.

In Jesus' name,
Amen.

Psalm 127:1-2

CONSISTENT HABIT

Dear God,

Help me discover how reasonably often I can write before running out of creative energy. Help me pace myself with this project but still allow myself to write consistently, whether that be six days a week, every other day, every two days, or once a week. Help me know my time and energy limitations as a writer and as a human being so that I can work with the limitations instead of trying to fight against them. Open up time for me to write. Thank You for the time You have given me to write, Lord. Help me make good use of it.

In Jesus' name,
Amen.

KNOWING THE FATHER'S LOVE IN THE WRITING PROCESS

Dear God,

Help me remember You're there throughout the process; show me what writing with You looks like. Help me be in tune with You constantly, knowing even in the back of my mind that You are here with me to support me, help me, show me Your love, and guide me. On this journey, let me begin to know Your character in beautiful, surprising ways. Thank You for being my father, Abba, and for letting me know I am not writing this project on my own but with Your perfect help and guidance. Help me have the passion and perseverance that I need to complete it. Let writing draw me closer to You. Let me know Your love better, heavenly Father. Bring glory to Your name in this. Thank You, Lord.

In Jesus' name,
Amen.

SELF-CARE AND SELF-DISCIPLINE

Dear God,

Give me divine inspiration and wisdom about my writing routine for this season. I want to be productive and healthy at the same time, having hobbies outside of writing and making time for people, too.

Help me take care of myself during the process of writing the book. Show me how to balance writing with my other responsibilities, too. Show me how to develop a healthy kind of self-discipline, sticking to a plan even when I might normally just want to distract myself with a number of things. Help me remember why I started writing. Let me glorify You in my day-by-day routine. Show me what that looks like.

In Jesus' name,
Amen.

DILIGENCE

Dear God,

Help me diligently use the gifts You have given me for Your glory. Lead me to helpful books on writing or revelations about the craft. Help me be smart about the writing process by putting thought into it and getting more done in less time instead of procrastinating and getting nothing done. Teach me excellence not only in the finished product, but also in the weekly process of writing. Help me find a healthy balance between everything I need to do and allow for rest. I want to let You into my whole day.

In Jesus' name,
Amen.

SAFE SPACE

Dear God,

Please help me find a safe space that I can go to and write, a place where I won't be disturbed, a place where I can find peace and quiet and healing. Please bring peace to this house, too. I don't know how You will do it, Lord, but I know it is possible for You to reconcile families and heal brokenness, or at the least, You provide relief from stress. Help me get away from the strife and write in peace. Bring healing to my family, friends, and neighborhood. Restore order. Thank You, Lord.

In Jesus' name,
Amen.

FICTION

ADVENTURE

Dear God,

Thank You for all the options in the world of stories for writers to write. You are infinite and wonderfully creative, and You have prepared storytellers to bring forth stories into the world since the beginning of time.

I want to write an adventure story of some kind. Lead me to a fitting setting for the story and an intriguing situation to explore. Help me find the fun elements of this story as I write it. Let the finished book be satisfying while revealing truth subtly. Let this bring glory to You.

In Jesus' name,
Amen.

FANTASY

Dear God,

You have created heaven, the universe, and earth. There is so much beauty and mystery to discover in what is real as well as in fantasy. I love the fantasy genre, and I think I can contribute something of value to it.

Help me create an interesting storyworld that is different from most fantasy worlds in a notable way. Show me what kind of storyworld would be most fitting for the book or series. How detailed a storyworld does it need to be?

Give me wisdom about the boundaries I should set for myself in terms of magic content. Help me see my own spiritual limitations. Lead me so that I don't go too far into the darker aspects of this world. If anything triggers anxiety for me, help me stay safe and find a healthy balance. Give me wisdom about this.

Help me reveal a glimpse of the beauty of the truth in this story. Show me the light of truth in reality so that I can bring it into this story.

Lord, show me what I can do differently with the fantasy genre so that it will be excellent and glorifying to You.

Give me a good story to write, Abba. Show me how to write it. I rely on You in this.

In Jesus' name,
Amen.

Psalm 104

SCIENCE FICTION/ SPECULATIVE

Dear God,

You carry far more understanding of the universe and of how everything works than anyone knows.

There is a question I want to explore using a science fiction or speculative fiction story. Show me how to flesh out characters, the rules of the world, the logic of the actions, and how to write the story in such a way that I'm not trying to convince the reader either way; instead, I'm presenting truths in a way that readers who ponder the story will come away with questions of their own and begin to seek the truth and find it. Give me wisdom in this process. Show me how to write an excellent book in this genre so that it brings glory to You. I rely on You in this.

In Jesus' name,
Amen.

MYSTERY

Dear God,

I want to write a compelling mystery that has a satisfying ending, a book that people will want to read over and over again. Please help me do that. Let me write something that is suspenseful and makes enough sense at the same time to suspend disbelief. Help me write interesting characters: an interesting main character, an interesting villain, and an interesting ally to the main character. Help me understand the motivations of the characters.

With the plot, Lord, show me how to string together the clues, riddles, and revelations in a way that makes sense and flows well so that there is not too much time between a question being posed and that same question being answered in the story. Show me how to set up a revelation skillfully so that it surprises readers but also makes sense.

Let me not glorify evil through my writing, Lord. Instead, let me subtly expose evil through the story in a way that causes readers to examine themselves and find correction.

In Jesus' name,
Amen.

ROMANCE

Dear God,

I'd like to write a romance novel, and I'd like it to be one that is true, noteworthy, satisfying, and very re-readable.

Help me write deep character arcs for each character in the romantic relationship. What do each of the characters need to learn over the course of this story, and how do I write that in a realistic and engaging way?

In the process of writing this story, teach me more about what a healthy, realistic relationship looks like and what it does not look like.

Let me not glorify unhealthy or unrealistic relationships in any way throughout this book. Expose any wrong ideas I hold about love, and lead me to the truth.

Lord, help me have fun writing this book. Help me care about my characters as they fall in love with each other. Help me discover the rhythms of their personalities — their mannerisms, their beliefs, and their habits. Help me portray these characters' personalities consistently throughout the book so that they become real to me.

Help me listen and hear what You have to say during the process. Help me also listen to the instincts and wisdom that You have given me to use in decision-making for this book. Give me discernment.

Thank You for this story idea. I'm really excited about it. And thank You for helping me with this project. Shape me into the image of Christ during the process of writing and releasing this book.

In Jesus' name,
Amen.

CONTEMPORARY

Dear God,

I'd like to write a contemporary book. Guide me in this. Lead me to the resources that will teach me what I need to know to write this book well. Give me wisdom for this story idea. Teach me how to write it. Let the end result be excellent in ways that glorify You. Help me develop my writing voice with this book and have fun in the process.

Thank You for being with me.

In Jesus' name,
Amen.

COMING OF AGE

Dear God,

I feel drawn to the coming of age genre. Help me discover the dynamics of the story. Show me how to write an effective, emotionally-satisfying story that helps Young readers feel less alone in their struggles. Give me understanding for this story.

Help me write honestly; show me how to write realistic characters that aren't all good or all bad.

Let the finished book be excellent in ways that glorify You. Thank You for helping me.

In Jesus' name,
Amen.

LITERARY

Dear God,

I would love to write a literary story. Give me wisdom and guide me if this is the right time and the right project for me to write. Lead me to resources that will teach me how to write an excellent literary book, one that causes me and readers to think differently in ways that lead us to truth. Teach me subtlety and the art of writing literary riddles through story like Jesus' parables. Teach me how to write a story that has multiple valid interpretations.

Teach me how to write prose
that is fitting for the book.

Thank You for helping me, Lord.

In Jesus' name,
Amen.

POETRY

Dear God,

I'd like to get into writing poetry. One doesn't really need to know much about poetry to begin playing around with words, I've heard.

I'm really looking forward to playing with words with You, Lord. Lead me to the resources that will help me develop a poetic voice and understand what makes poetry sing. I receive wisdom from You, too, Lord, because You offer it to me generously.

You're indescribable, more beautiful than any language can say. Thank You for revealing Yourself to me.

In Jesus' name,
Amen.

NONFICTION

MEMOIR

Dear God,

I have an amazing testimony to share, and I believe I should share it in a memoir, but I also need guidance. Some of my story is very sensitive to me now, and I don't know if I'm ready to share everything in this book. Help me decide what to leave in and what to leave out when it comes to my life, and how to treat sensitive information. Should I use real names or fake names for people I know? Lead me each step of the way in writing this book, Lord. Thank You for watching over me my whole life. Let Christ's love and wisdom illuminate my life story as I write it. Let me recognize more and more truths within my testimony as the words flow from my fingertips.

My life is Yours. Here I am.

In Jesus' name,
Amen.

SELF-HELP

Dear God,

There's something important that I want to share with the world. Give me wisdom as to whether this is something I have enough knowledge about to write.

If I'm the right person to write this book, lead me in your perfect timing to write it, whether it be now or several years down the line. Let it be full of truth, written beautifully with no misguided ideas. If there is anything false in it, Lord, please correct me and lead me to the truth.

I want to write accurately and truthfully in a way that helps people. Please teach me how to write coherently and organize each topic in a way that flows well and makes sense.

Continue to teach me the truth, Lord, and if there is anything that needs to change within me during the process of writing this book, please transform me. I'm open to Your correction, Lord. Let Your will be done in me. Thank You for leading me to write.

In Jesus' name,
Amen.

THEOLOGY

Dear God,

I feel called to write a theological book. Give me wisdom about this idea. Help me develop it. Help me meet You in this process, Lord, and help me lead others closer to You through the wisdom You teach me. I'm open to You.

Lead me to accurate sources for the research process. Show me what is noteworthy to write about in this book.

How do I write a book that shows readers that You are so wonderful and worthy of worship? Lead me through the process of writing this book with You. Write through me. Reveal Your heart to me and show me how to communicate in the book more about You than readers knew before. Let Your will be done in me and in this book as it is in heaven.

In Jesus' name,
Amen.

CHARACTERS

BEGINNING WORK

Dear God,

You are the most creative being, and You want to be involved in my writing process. Please bring characters to my imagination for this story that fit. Help me imagine how they look and act, how they talk, what they wear, and how they move. Let them light up the story and add to the richness of the storyworld. Show me ideas of things they might struggle with. Give me understanding of what their roles are in the storyworld; let me see how they interact with different people.

Guide me on this process of discovery; help me recognize the most important characters to focus on. Give me discernment to write realistic character arcs for them.

Help me enjoy this part of the writing process.

In Jesus' name,
Amen.

MAIN CHARACTER

Dear God,

How do I make my main character for this adventure story more distinctive and believable? I really want to make an intriguing, relatable hero who surprises the reader with his actions in ways that make sense considering who he is. Let him be someone the reader will want to win against the villain. Help me make both the hero and villain interesting and fully rounded.

How do I make my hero just as interesting, if not more so, than the villain? I would like to give my hero an internal struggle that influences the plot in some way, and I would like to show how he overcomes that struggle, or at least makes progress towards overcoming it. Help me understand this hero well enough so that I can write his decisions organically and not force them for the sake of the plot. I already love this character. Let the hero come alive in my imagination so that once the final draft is revised and edited, the readers will love him too.

In Jesus' name,
Amen.

ANTAGONIST

Dear God,

Does this story have an antagonist in it, someone who opposes what the main character wants to do? The antagonist might not even be completely evil. He might be someone who thinks he is doing the right thing and he might not even do evil things. Or he might be mostly evil and selfish and unwilling to change. If so, help me understand this character. At the same time, help me separate myself from him in my head to a healthy extent.

Give me wisdom about what this particular story needs from the character. Who is this antagonist? What does he want? I'll write down the ideas for it that I've got in my head.

Thank You, Lord, for listening. I will be still and listen to You now.

In Jesus' name,
Amen.

HOW MANY CHARACTERS

Dear God,

Give me wisdom about the amount of characters in the book. Are there any characters in it that I can take out of the book to strengthen the story? Maybe a character I really like actually belongs in a different book I haven't written yet. Help me make good decisions. Also, if the book is missing any characters who would strengthen the story, bring them to my imagination and show me how to weave them into it.

In Jesus' name,
Amen.

POINT-OF-VIEW

Dear God,

I'm trying to find out which character's point-of-view would be the most interesting or meaningful one for this book. Or which two or three characters' points-of-view, if that would be more helpful in telling the whole story. Teach me how to weave the tale's tapestry of characters together.

What do You see in my characters? What do You see in me that might be coming out in my characters unconsciously? What can I learn from this in my personal life and my self-improvement journey? Show me what You see. Give me wisdom.

In Jesus' name,
Amen.

MOTIVATION

Dear God,

What does this character want? Why does she want it? I don't know how to figure this out. How do You see this character, Lord? What am I not seeing yet? Help me understand this character better and make her feel like a real person. Let her also be a character who brings surprising, theme-fitting life and depth to the book.

In Jesus' name,
Amen.

OUTLINING

PLAN OF ACTION

Dear God,

Out of all the elements I could develop first, including character, setting, and the main questions of the plot, what should I form as the ground on which to develop the others? Or, what are the core things that I need to know about this story first? I know in the writing process things may change, but help me find the things that will not change in the course of writing this story, whether it's a character who shows up vividly to me or a storyworld that is very developed. How has the storyworld and its cultures influenced my characters as they grew up? Help me write this in an organic way that is consistent with my worldbuilding. Help me sense Your guidance, Lord. Thank You for hearing me.

In Jesus' name,
Amen.

SMALL, DOABLE STEPS

Dear God,

Please help me break this project into small, doable steps so that I'm not overwhelmed with this whole project. Help me know what to work on today, and then tomorrow.

Let organization help and not hinder my creative process. Lead me each step of the way with inspiration, hope, and perseverance. Thank You, Lord, for being a part of this project and helping me.

Let your name be glorified.

In Jesus' name,
Amen.

BEGINNING

Dear God,

I want to write an effective, satisfying, and fitting beginning to this book, one that is well-written, one that makes promises about the story that I can and will keep. Give me wisdom about how to introduce the characters, when to introduce them, and in what order. Show me how and when to introduce the theme or allude to its nature subtly. Help me choose a good first sentence. I don't want to overwhelm the readers with too much exposition or too many questions. And then help me know what the second scene should focus on and why. How do I write a good follow-up scene to the beginning?

Show me Your perspective on excellent beginnings. Give me wisdom about the book as a whole and its story structure. Help me understand my story and where it fits on the scale between action-driven and character-driven stories. Help me think clearly and learn discernment for what this story needs.

In Jesus' name,
Amen.

MIDDLE

Dear God,

Help me write an engaging middle to this book. Let it all make sense and not go all over the place. Allow me to write an intriguing middle that continues to satisfy me and the reader, building upon the promises I made in the beginning. Let there be well-formed surprises. Let there be wonderful moments between the characters. Let there be funny parts, too, if humor fits the tone of the story. Help me balance the tone so that it is just right for what the book needs to be. Help me shape the book. Shape me, too, in the process. Thank You for being a part of this journey, Lord.

In Jesus' name,
Amen.

END

Dear God,

Give me inspiration and understanding for the ending of this book. What should happen? What should the last sentence be? Help me write an ending that is worthy of its beginning and middle. My goal is to write an ending that is satisfying in itself while making the rest of the book good too, if not better than before.

Guide me, loving Father. Thank You for everything.

In Jesus' name,
Amen.

THEME

Dear God,

What are some possible themes or issues and truths that will be explored in this story? How might I write these themes ambiguously enough, without preaching through the characters, but letting characters think for themselves and letting things happen naturally as they might unfold in real life? How do I handle this particular story?

Help me understand if this book is meant to ask people profound questions and get them thinking, or if this book's purpose is to reveal answers when it comes to its theme. Should the ending of the book be open and uncertain, or should it be resolved? Teach me how to write the book as it needs to be written.

In Jesus' name,
Amen.

HEART OF THE BOOK

Dear God,

Help me identify the heart of the book You have given me to write, whether it is strong or weak or just an idea right now. Show me how to strengthen it and portray it through the story in a beautiful way. And if I don't need to know the theme of the book at this point in the process, give me peace.

Thank You, Lord, for Your peace.

In Jesus' name,
Amen.

INSECURITIES

ASSURANCE

Dear God,

I need validation that this book has enough value for me to write it and that You would be happy with me writing it with You. Please give me this assurance and let me throw out all doubts that try to tell me otherwise. Help me get rid of everything that keeps me from writing the book and from writing it excellently. Shape me today, Lord, as You will. You are understanding and loving. Thank You for Your friendship.

In Jesus' name,
Amen.

SELF-CRITICISM

Dear God,

Help me to be kind to myself in the writing process, not hating myself and not hating the stories You have put inside of me but accepting myself where I am as a person and as a writer and accepting my stories. Help me to not criticize my writing in the early stages or allow others to criticize it in the early stages too much so that I can have a safe place to create and play in peace. Help me enjoy the writing process, not expecting it to be unpleasant because of the harsh experiences of other writers, but expecting it to be fun, meaningful, and that it will draw me closer to You.

Help me to not be mean to myself and my writing. Help me recognize harmful self-talk and stop. I want to become an emotionally healthier person. Show me how to look at myself and my writing without judgment. Teach me how to encourage myself.

You understand things far better than I can, Yahweh, and You are merciful. Teach me mercy. Teach me how to see with clear perspective, logic, positive creativity, understanding, and love.

In Jesus' name,
Amen.

ABILITY

Dear God,

I'm overwhelmed. This project is big, and I don't know how I'm going to do it justice, let alone finish it. Please give me peace and help me keep going if this is a good project to finish. I know that sometimes, overwhelming projects are worth finishing, but am I ready to write this one? Maybe there's another, easier project or several small projects I can write first that will help me learn how to write this one later on in my life. Guide me with Your wisdom, Lord, and lead me into excellent counsel.

In Jesus' name,
Amen.

VALUE

Dear God,

Help me give weight to this book, believing it is valuable even if it doesn't change everyone's lives significantly. Help me treasure this book and not take it for granted. Thank You for giving it to me, Lord. Help me be a good steward of the project as I write it. Help me be faithful in this work. Thank You for hearing me, Lord. Do what You will within me.

In Jesus' name,
Amen.

TIMING

Dear God,

Help me understand where Your timing is in all this. I'll keep working on the book in faith that You want me to keep writing. Help me know when to set my goals for finishing this book or if I should let this work take years for me to write. I really don't know, Lord. Give me wisdom and sense to keep doing what You want me to do while I wait for You to bring clearer answers to me.

If this is something that You're leaving up to me, Lord, and if it is something that You don't have a specific timeline for, give me wisdom about having a healthy balance between writing and living life so that I can live healthily as I write the book. Thank You for hearing me. Thank You for loving me and shaping me into who You want me to be.

In Jesus' name,
Amen.

TIMING CONTINUED

Dear God,

I still don't know how long I should take to write this book, and I haven't gotten a clear answer from You. Is that something I should know, or should I just keep working on it and set my own goals? I know that if I took more time than I was planning to take on this book, I could improve it, but I really want to finish this soon. More than that, I feel like I need to finish this book soon, before I run out of steam and discount the importance of it. I feel like I need to get it into the world. It's not perfect; it will never be perfect. It might be good enough, though, soon, especially with Your help, Lord. Help me understand Your will. Let Your will be done in me.

In Jesus' name,
Amen.

STUCK

WRITER'S BLOCK

Dear God,

Help me work through writer's block. Help me understand what's keeping me from writing, whether it be fear, or perfectionism, or something else, and help me overcome it. If I need exercise, make a way for me to get exercise, whether by myself or with a friend. If I need to get some sleep and not think about the book for a day or two, let me know and help me have grace and patience with myself. Direct my mind to what I should do today. Help me tune in to Your presence and to the Holy Spirit who comforts and gives wisdom.

I remember that this is something many writers go through and overcome. I can make it through this, too, and I want to do it with You.

In Jesus' name,
Amen.

INDECISION

Dear God,

I don't know what to work on today. This is a problem I have a lot — I just don't know where to start, even though I have a to-do list and several things I could be doing. Give me ideas of what to do in the future when I'm not sure what to work on. I know I should probably have a set schedule and plan, but I'm more of a spontaneous person than a planner. Still, I'll trust You will give me wisdom to plan. It's hard to commit to a decision for a day, but maybe I should work towards learning how to commit to a choice of what I'm going to work on for the day. Guide me, Lord. Help me become less indecisive as I draw closer to You. I rely on You for guidance for today.

Thank You for who You are.

In Jesus' name,
Amen.

UNSURE

Dear God,

There's something wrong with this story, but I can't put my finger on what it is. I'm not sure what to do about it. Please, help me identify what exactly is wrong. You know everything that's going on in the book — including what I'm sensing — and how to fix it. Let me see the story from a new angle and notice the specific problem with it. Show me how You see it.

Thank You so much, God, for Your involvement in my creative life. Let this be an opportunity for me to learn something and grow as a writer on my journey to knowing You better. Let Your name be glorified in this, and let my relationship with You strengthen because of this journey.

In Jesus' name,
Amen.

BORED

Dear God,

I'll admit it, the story has gotten boring for me. Please give me wisdom on how to make it interesting or exciting or intriguing or whatever it needs to be so that I'm excited about it again. I really want it to be a good book. Help me allow myself to get excited about it and invest in it emotionally. Shape this book, Lord. Shape me in the process of writing it. Thank You so much for helping me.

In Jesus' name,
Amen.

PLOT

Dear God,

I'm stuck. Where should I go from here? Please, help me get unstuck. Give me ideas of what to do. Help me get this plot unstuck. What should the characters do next? How are they going to solve this problem? Deep breath. Thank You, Lord, for giving me this book. Thank You for leading me this far. Thank You for teaching me what to do when I'm stuck. I give this to You. Thank You for being a part of my writing process and leading me to a really good version of this story while transforming me into who You want me to be.

In Jesus' name,
Amen.

OUTLINE

Dear God,

Please help me keep going, even though I feel stuck. If I need to outline something with more detail, whether it's a specific scene or one of the acts, give me wisdom about it. Help me envision the story as a cohesive whole in my head, playing it out and seeing what is beautiful about it. Let me see the story from an angle that gives me the inspiration I need to keep writing.

Thank You for being a part of this process, God, even when it's not fun. Thank You for hearing me. You want to be a part of this process even when I don't quite understand it. You love me a lot more than I know. Thank You for helping me with this story. I'm relying on You.

In Jesus' name,
Amen.

THE STRUGGLE IS REAL

Dear God,

I'm just kind of stuck, but I feel like I should take a break from writing this book for a while. Should I wait a few weeks or months? A few years? Give me wisdom. Help me have peace about it. Give me wisdom about whether to work on another book during this downtime, too, or if I shouldn't work on this genre for a while. Thank You for letting me know it's okay to take a break, Lord.

In Jesus' name,
Amen.

UNMOTIVATED

Dear God,

Today, I'm just not motivated to write. I'm not sure if it's burn-out from writing a lot, or if life stuff is getting in the way of my energy levels, or something else. Maybe I'm bored with the book. Help me see what's wrong, God. Let me see it with eyes of wonder, knowing that writing this story is a gift. Let me imagine it in a beautiful and interesting way, not a dull way, and let me know You'll give me the words to write. Please, help me get to the place where I can work on it with joy, enthusiasm, and perseverance. I want to worship You with this book.

Let me learn something from this day, even if it's something small. Show me how You see it. Thank You for being involved in my creative process and all areas of my life. Let me bring glory to You today.

In Jesus' name,
Amen.

LOST CREATIVE JOY

Dear God,

I think I've lost my joy in writing. Please, please help me regain it. Help me see beauty and purpose and meaning in my writing. Help me remember the times that I have really enjoyed writing and when it was satisfying for me. It's hard for me to believe that this is important and that I can do it and enjoy it.

Thinking more about it, I think it's related to something else. Maybe I'm mourning over something horrible that happened. Circumstances have come up that have made writing seem dull.

Give me Your perspective. Let me know that this is not the end of my writing journey, and that I can find joy in writing again. Please help me, God. I give this over to You because You care about it even more than I do. Heal what is broken within me and renew my hope and joy, beginning with You. Then, awaken within me the thrill of stories and writing prose, when thinking of my characters and themes. Remind me that writing truly is a beautiful and worthwhile thing, and that it's something I can do with love and joy, even if only for myself or someone dear to me. Glorify Your name, Lord.

In Jesus' name,
Amen.

VALUE

Dear God,

I feel like I have been dismissing the importance of my own writing because of the fear that in the end it won't be satisfying, whether or not it finds an audience. Give me wisdom. Help me value my writing. Let me see how much You value this. This is important to You, God. You gave me this gift and desire for a reason. It does matter. I'll write something today, even if it's something small. Writing takes faith. Thank You for this project, Lord. Teach me to value writing and tell myself that it is valid and important because I care about it a lot. Help me see how You value me, too. Thank You for Your presence, Jesus. Thank You for hearing me and answering me. Thank You for Your love.

In Jesus' name,
Amen.

REASON FOR WRITING

Dear God,

Why do I write in the first place? What is so deep inside me that I have to get out with words? Please guide me and remind me why I started this project.

In Jesus' name,
Amen.

WRITING THE FIRST DRAFT

FIRST DRAFT

Dear God,

Help me be patient with myself in writing this draft. I know it won't be perfect in the beginning. Help me give myself permission to write however I need to write to get this draft finished. Perseverance to the end of this first draft matters the most right now. Give me peace, knowing that in the end it will be a good book and that it is okay for this draft to be bad, terrible even. Help me persevere to the end of this draft and see that it's not so bad and that You will help me make it better. Remind me that You are committed to helping me with anything that I bring to You. Thank You so much for Your grace and support, Father God. Let me glorify You by my perseverance and by relying on You in this process. I give this to You.

In Jesus' name,
Amen.

PROTECTION

Dear God,

While I am writing this book, protect me. Protect me from the doubts that would keep me from writing this book or delay the process. Protect me from all harm.

Lead me away from anything that is evil, Lord, and break off any bondage that might cause spiritual attack. If I need a professional counselor or spiritual leader, let me know and lead me to the right one who will help me with this.

Thank You, God, for protecting me and leading me to safety in Your presence and right way of living.

Give me wisdom about who I should keep close in my life and who I should distance myself from, and give me peace about it. Help me take careful and effective steps to slowly or abruptly distance myself from dangerous or abusive people in my life; protect me from them.

Protect me in my house and protect me on the roads.

Help me have faith in You for safety for myself, and for my family and people I care deeply about.

Help me know I am safe and that
Your angels are protecting me.

Help me know my prayers are enough, that You
hear my prayers and that You are helping me even
when I don't know if I have enough faith. Help me
know my faith is enough, even when it flickers.

Help me know how weak the enemy is. Help
me see how strong I am in You, Lord of
love. Let me grow strong in You, Abba.

Deliver me from temptation and
from evil. Purify me.

Baptize my imagination and all
other senses in Your peace, love,
deliverance, and divine inspiration.

Protect my computers, my journal, my writing
utensils and tools, and all my books.

Protect my work in progress from its beginning
to its end, and protect it as it goes into
publication; protect it as it goes into the world.

Protect me from all evil spirits.

Protect me from myself.

Keep me from going away from You, Lord.

Keep me from doing the worst things.

Protect my sleep, Lord.

Protect my dreams, God.

Protect my identity.

Protect my heart.

Protect my mind.

Protect my body.

Protect my family.

Protect my friends.

Protect me from giving in to harmful doubt.

Protect me from nightmares.

Help my prayers become more effective and wise.

Help my faith, God.

Help me guard my heart wisely.

Thank You for helping me pray. This is going to change my life.

In Jesus' name,
Amen.

MEANING AND MYSTERY

Dear God,

I have heard it said by several people that I should not try to understand what my story means till it is finished, and even then, that it is best not to limit interpretations of it. Help me understand what this means and whether or not this is good advice for me.

If this is best for me, help me not try to figure out all that this story means until it is done and I can read it from the eyes of a reader. Let me experience the story first and foremost as a story and not as a sermon, though truth should come through it. Even then, let there be an element of mystery to the book; let me know simply that in this story there is profound truth and I can be content.

Let this story be bigger than me. Let that cause me to respect this story, to respect its mysterious meanings, by not allowing myself to pigeonhole the book but to open myself up to surprises. Surprise me in the writing process, Lord, and help me accept the truths that come through the book. In this way, help me develop genuine humility. I trust in You, and I know that I don't know very much in this huge universe after all.

In Jesus' name,
Amen.

A DAY TO OUTLINE

Dear God,

Today, I'm outlining this project for an hour. Guide me through the process. It will be fun. Let every frustrating section of the project that comes up be another opportunity for me to lean on You, learn, and stretch my creativity. Maybe even stretch my faith. I will trust You in this. Thank You for outlining with me today, Lord. Show me how detailed or how vague the outline can be so that when I write the draft, there will still be enough mystery for me to enjoy writing it and bring a fresh experience to its pages.

In Jesus' name,
Amen.

DISTRACTIONS

Dear God,

Clear away the distractions from my life so that I can focus on writing. Show me what I need to remove from my daily life, at least temporarily, till I finish this book. Cleanse my life of meaningless clutter. In its place, help me find a healthier way to write uninterrupted for longer amounts of time while still getting enough sleep at night. Help me find places to go where I can write uninterrupted. Give me the motivation to actually go to those places and write regularly if I need a new location to be productive. Thank You, Lord, for hearing me.

In Jesus' name,
Amen.

GRATITUDE

Dear God,

Thank You so much for the story You have given me. It is dear to my heart, and I'm thankful that I'm able to work on it right now. Thank You for the characters. They mean a lot to me, and they help me remember why I write. Thank You for the theme. Thank You for the writing abilities You have given me. Thank You for giving me reasons to write. Thank You for the time You have given me to write. Thank You for giving me these wonderful ideas, and thank You for giving me the words to say them with.

Thank You for my family, and thank You for life today. Thank You for using me today. Thank You for bringing glory to Yourself through me and through this story. Thank You for giving me an eye and an ear for story. Thank You for helping me become a better writer and a more considerate person. Thank You for helping me experience Your love and peace today. Thank You for helping me allow your love to spread to the people around me.

In Jesus' name,
Amen.

A DAY TO WRITE

Dear God,

Today I will write, and I invite You to collaborate with me on this project. I will rely on You for the ideas I need today. Thank You for Your provision and for this opportunity to write. Let the words come easily, Lord. Thank You for letting me be close to You and learn from Your infinite creativity. Hallelujah! The very thought of this excites me.

In Jesus' name,
Amen.

Psalm 45:1

FRUSTRATED

Dear God,

I'm frustrated right now because I want to be more productive than I have been, but I feel like I'm always being distracted or interrupted. Help me figure out how to remedy this. I give this to You and choose to listen to the Holy Spirit. I choose to stop worrying about this because the book is in Your hands. I trust You to guide me this month about the book.

In Jesus' name,
Amen.

WRITING ONE CHAPTER

Dear God,

Today, I aim to write a chapter in the book, and I'm looking forward to writing it. It's a fun chapter. Thank You, Lord, for being with me. This is exciting. Okay. Here we go.

In Jesus' name,
Amen.

LETTING GO OF CONTROL

Dear God,

There's a desperate feeling I get sometimes. The feeling is that I have to control the story or else I'll get it wrong, but writing doesn't always work that way. Help me let this story be what it is, Lord. Help me hold my opinions and plans loosely enough, allowing surprises into the writing process and allowing the characters to learn in an organic way over the course of the story. Help me to not force anything, but let whatever truth is in the story come out of it naturally. Help me find balance between play and structure so that the story falls into place and it's easy to write drafts. Shape me as You inspire me, and help me decide which paths to take. Let Your name be glorified.

In Jesus' name,
Amen.

TITLE

Dear God,

Today, I'm trying to figure out a title for this project. Please help me find a really good one. I'm looking for one that stands out but also fits what the book is about. A title that paints a picture for the reader but also leaves a question of what the work is about.

I'm so thankful You're excited about this project and want to help me. Okay. Please let me find the title soon. I give this to You, Lord. Thank You for being part of my creative process. Thank You for hearing me and helping me.

In Jesus' name,
Amen.

PATIENCE WITH MYSELF

Dear God,

Help me be patient with myself today. I distracted myself and just never got around to writing. Help me accept myself where I am, and help me to take my current struggle to focus into account when it comes to getting words written. Maybe if I lower my expectations of how much I want to write or how well I think I should write initially, I will be able to write at least one sentence today. Help me lower my expectations of myself so that I don't get so stressed about this first draft. Let me feel Your peace.

Thank you. <3

In Jesus' name,
Amen.

DETERMINATION

Dear God,

I'm so determined to write a good book. Help me keep this determination, this energy, this fire. Let it not go out.

Today, I will write a lot.

Today, I will write in a satisfying way.

Today, I will have fun writing.

Today, I will write with passion.

Let me write a book that reflects a lot of light, a book that is used by its readers like a nightlight. Show me how.

In Jesus' name,
Amen.

A FULL DAY

Dear God,

Today has been a satisfyingly full day of productivity. Thank You for helping me write.

In Jesus' name,
Amen.

A DAY OF WRITING

Dear God,

Thank You for this new day. I'm going to write a lot today for a specific set time. I'm feeling laid back and excited about it. I feel as though I'm beginning to get the hang of a writing routine. Thank You, Lord. I tune myself in to You and trust that You are guiding me. I'm ready to discover the creative words and imagery that belong in this story. Thank You, Yahweh, for helping me grow in my creative skills.

In Jesus' name,
Amen.

WRITING MUSIC PLAYLIST

Dear God,

Help me find the perfect songs for my storyworld, my characters, my story's aesthetic and situations. Help me put together a playlist that will inspire me to write in the story whenever I listen to the songs, one that won't distract me while I'm writing; one that gives me ideas for the story that I'm working on. Let the songs have the right tone for what I'm writing.

In Jesus' name,
Amen.

PERSONAL TRANSFORMATION

Dear God,

How is this book changing me? Am I drawing closer to You or further from You? Am I becoming a more loving person, or am I becoming more irritable? And lastly, am I cultivating faith or hope inside of me while writing this story? Or am I feeding an unhealthy cynicism? Yahweh, help me understand what this book is teaching and reminding me. Help me know if it is good. Show me if anything I have plotted out for the story should be changed, or if there is anything about the way I write that should be changed. If so, lead me and give me the necessary patience and willingness to shift my way of thinking. Help me develop the confidence and endurance I need to continue writing. Let Your will be done in me as it is in heaven. Transform me with Your healing love into the image of Christ. Let this positive transformation influence what I write and how I write. Let this bring glory to You.

In Jesus' name,
Amen.

Psalm 139

FINISHED THE ROUGH DRAFT

Dear God,

I am so, so excited. I just finished the rough draft and put "The End" at the end! This is so satisfying. Thank You for helping me through this writing process.

Now I'll give it some time before rereading it and beginning the rewriting process. To be honest, I'm not looking forward to seeing the flaws in the work, but I'm thankful that I have the tools I need to improve it with time.

I give this draft to You.

In Jesus' name,
Amen.

REWRITING

READING FIRST DRAFT

Dear God,

Today, I'm reading the rough draft after letting it sit for a while. Help me not cringe too much. And teach me what to look for. Point out things to me that I can learn from, Lord, and help me gain new vision of what I can do better in the next draft. Continue to shape me and give me patience with myself and with the book. Thank You for being with me in this.

In Jesus' name,
Amen.

IMPROVEMENT

Dear God,

This book could be improved. A lot. Help me not burn this draft in fury and give up.

Lord, help me see what to change and how to change it so that each part of the book is excellent in Your eyes. Guide my hands, my mind, and my heart as I work on the book. Show me how You view storytelling. Help me see from Your perspective what is good and what can be improved when it comes to the way that I write and my heart behind writing.

In Jesus' name,
Amen.

REWRITE

Dear God,

Today, I'm working on another draft of the book. Give me vision for what to focus on in this rewrite.

In Jesus' name,
Amen.

LIMITED PERFECTION

Dear God,

Thank You for helping me see that the book doesn't have to be the best book in the world. It doesn't even have to be brilliant. No story is perfect but Yours, and Your story is infinite. You use imperfect things for Your own glory, Lord, and that's beautiful. Please, use this story for Your glory, and help me make it good enough, if not better.

In Jesus' name,
Amen.

REVISION & EDITING

EDITING

Dear God,

Today, I'm working on editing the book. Give me wisdom about how to go about that. Right now, I'm just going through and looking at it and fixing whatever I see that needs fixing, but later I'll go through it intentionally to edit dialogue specifically, and then another time I'll go through it to specifically edit prose, and so on. Help me notice mistakes; give me wisdom to make sentences more effective. Help me decide between different versions of a sentence, Lord, and help me see it in the context of the paragraph it is in. Show me how to decide between different versions of a scene, too.

In Jesus' name,
Amen.

WORDS

Dear God,

I feel like many of the words in this scene don't describe the setting or the action very well. Help me see the story the way You see it. Let me imagine the scene I'm writing in the most intriguing way imaginable, and help me translate it into really good words. Give me a vocabulary of accurate words and phrases for each chapter in this book and the ability to see how to best arrange them into paragraphs. And then give me wisdom about how to arrange those paragraphs progressively so that it keeps the readers' attention and satisfies me when I read it back to myself.

Sometimes it's hard for me to look at my book and appreciate it. But as I'm reading through it, there are a few sentences in this scene that I'm happy with. And I really like this bit of dialogue between my two main characters. At least I have that. I hope I'll be able to keep those words in the final draft, that they still fit.

Give me wisdom on how to balance prose and dialogue appropriately for this scene. You care about that kind of thing too because it points back to excellence. Help me edit this and make it excellent so that it glorifies You, Lord.

Thank You so much, God, for being in this writing process with me. I'm not doing this alone; You are doing this with me and guiding me, even in ways I might not be noticing. Thank You so much, Lord.

In Jesus' name,
Amen.

DECISION-MAKING

Dear God,

I'm moving right along. Thank You for helping me make progress. This isn't too bad. Well, some of it is tedious, but some of it is fun. The part that is the most tedious is when it's hard to decide between two different versions of a scene, or two different versions of a sentence or paragraph. Sometimes, it's really hard. I might even like both versions of a sentence or paragraph or scene for different reasons, but which one fits the best in this place in the book? Give me discernment and understanding. Help me not make decisions out of frustration and impatience or fear, but out of wisdom, reasoning, preference, and peace. Thank You, Abba. I really need this.

In Jesus' name,
Amen.

THE FINAL EDITS

NEAR THE END

Dear God,

Writing this book has been a long journey. I'm looking forward to being able to say it's done. Help me enjoy writing the end. Help me not let insecurities get in the way of doing the work.

In Jesus' name,
Amen.

CALLING IT DONE

Dear God,

After today, I'm calling the book done. There's a lot more I could do with it, but that will always be true no matter how much I work on it. Give me peace about finishing. I feel like it's time and that it is good. It's the best I can do right now. Direct me to whatever last-minute changes I need to make before sending this book out into the world. Thank You for helping me, Lord. Guide me to the next project after this, and give me new joy. It's hard to let go of a project.

In Jesus' name,
Amen.

THANK YOU

Dear God,

Thank You for the book. It's finished. That in itself is a miracle. Thank You for leading me the whole way and helping me get back into writing when I had tough days. Thank You so much. The book means a lot to me, and I hope it will be meaningful to someone else, too. Thank You, Lord, for being with me like always, whether I notice it or not. Thank You for helping me find beauty in the process.

In Jesus' name,
Amen.

PART II
PUBLISHING

DEAR GOD,

Give me a peace that surpasses understanding, wisdom for today, and the ability to get things done peacefully and in a timely manner. I receive this with faith.

In Jesus' name,
Amen.

THE DECISION

RIGHT PERSPECTIVE

Dear God,

I really, really want to be published, but I don't know if the reason for this desire is merely so that people will notice me. Am I at peace if only a few people ever read my work and are touched by it? Help me have the right perspective about getting my book published. Help me humble myself and know that no matter what happens, I have finished a book, and simply the process of writing it has changed my life for the better, and that pleases You. Show me how You see this. I give this to You. Let Your will be done in me as it is in heaven.

In Jesus' name,
Amen.

PEACE

Dear God,

Help me be at peace about actually publishing my book, if that's what You want me to do. Help me have peace about the future of this book and not worry about it having too few readers, suddenly becoming popular, or getting lots of negative reviews. Give me wisdom, too, and help me give up these burdens. Thank You, God, for giving me this book. Thank You for staying with me in all of this and never leaving me. Thank You for being my greatest advocate. I will trust You and give up these burdens.

In Jesus' name,
Amen.

CONFIRMATION

Dear God,

Thank You for the confirmation You gave me today for publishing the book. Thank You so much. Now I don't have any excuse for procrastinating on it. Thank You. I'll get back to work on the book.

In Jesus' name,
Amen.

PREPARATION

FOCUS

Dear God,

Help me focus on what I'm doing, not on what others are doing, so that I can be faithful to the work and have a sound mind.

In Jesus' name,
Amen.

WHEN TO PUBLISH

Dear God,

Give me wisdom about when to publish this book. Should I do it right away or wait? If I should wait, show me how long I should wait before trying to publish, whether traditionally or by myself. Should I write more drafts of this book first? If so, give me the peace, endurance, and perseverance that I need. If I should stop rewriting, help me to stop, accept the book, and let it go into the world.

In Jesus' name,
Amen.

READERS

Dear God,

Please show me who my target audience is. I pray that the people the book is for get ahold of my book and read the whole thing. I pray that the book cover, title, and synopsis all catch their attention, and they get excited to read the book. I pray that when they read it, it will be even more satisfying to them than they were expecting. I pray that they will tell their friends about the book, and that those friends won't dismiss it as just another book. As they hear about my book, help them be interested enough to pick it up and begin reading it.

Help me treat my readers like real people, even while I'm marketing the book. Help me be the kind of author whom readers love talking about and looking up to. Help me truly have good character and the ability to connect with people. Help me be the people person that my readers need, even if I never meet the readers face-to-face.

Help me treat my fans with genuine love, respect, and patience.

Show me the best ways to get my books into the hands of the readers who will be touched by it.

In Jesus' name,
Amen.

MAKING THE BOOK READY

Dear God,

Help me only release the book when it's ready. In the age of self-publishing, I can make anything into a book to sell, and that is a huge responsibility.

How many rounds of edits will this book need? What parts need to be strengthened the most? How will I know when I'm done?

I give this all to You, Lord. I bow before You and give it up to You.

You are beautiful and good, and You work out things for the good of those who love You. You are patient. You are kind. Thank You.

In Jesus' name,
Amen.

READERS PART II

Dear God,

I think I understand a little better now who my audience is. Of course, it might turn out differently than I expect, but it's nice to have an idea of who would probably like this book the most. Thank You, Lord. I have a little bit of closure now, and I feel like I can move forward with a little more confidence. Let Your will be done in this house as it is in heaven.

In Jesus' name,
Amen.

WRITING THE INTRODUCTION (NONFICTION)

Dear God,

Not every book needs an introduction, but I think this nonfiction project needs one. Give me the wisdom and discernment to introduce the book to readers in a way that is interesting and easy to read. Help me know what is most important for me to write about concerning the book — be it the story behind it, the reason for the book, what the book is about, the way the book is ordered, the way the book can be used, or anything else. I don't want to write so much that readers don't even get to the main part of the book before they quit reading. Help me find a balance, Lord.

In Jesus' name,
Amen.

WRITING ACKNOWLEDGMENTS

Dear God,

Who do I want to mention in the acknowledgments? There are so many people I would like to mention who didn't even help me with the writing process. And I don't want to mention someone just because I feel like I should. I want to acknowledge the people who contributed the most, but also the people who encouraged me. Without them, this book wouldn't be here.

Talking through this with You is helping, Lord. Thank You for listening to me.

In Jesus' name,
Amen.

SELF-PUBLISHING OR TRADITIONAL PUBLISHING

Dear God,

I ask for guidance about publishing. Help me know whether it would be better for this book to be self-published or traditionally published.

If it is to be traditionally published, guide me through the process and lead me to the right people who will help me through the process smoothly. Let us work together in harmony, and help me understand the contract. Let the final contract be beneficial and appropriate for my project.

If it is to be self-published, lead me through each step with peace and patience, and help me know how to manage each part of the process. Bring the right people into my life to help me, and help me recognize them when they come. Help me walk in love in all situations. No matter which way I choose, help the finished result of the book be enough.

In Jesus' name,
Amen.

TRADITIONAL

RIGHT AGENT

Dear God,

I feel drawn to traditional publishing, so I'm going to follow that path unless something changes. Please show me which agent to go with and give me discernment so that I choose the right kind of agent and not one who will rip me off. Give me peace about the right one. Help me know the questions to ask when interviewing the agent. Allow us to work well together. Guide all of our interactions. Thank You, God, for this opportunity.

In Jesus' name,
Amen.

SUBMITTING

Dear God,

Okay. I have found a possible agent and done my research; I'm submitting my query today. I give this to You. Thank You for getting me this far, Lord. If the work is ready, and if this is the right person, let this be accepted.

In Jesus' name,
Amen.

WAITING

Dear God,

Give me wisdom of what to do while I wait for the results of my submission, whether it gets accepted or rejected. Help me have peace and patience in this time frame and know that it's going to be okay no matter what happens. Work behind the scenes and grant me favor. If this gets rejected, help me get back up again and become a stronger writer. Show me what can be improved in this piece. Give me the courage to submit the query to someone else. If this gets accepted, help me accept success, whether it is little or big. Help me respond with healthy humility, remembering my true source of value. Then I will work away at what needs to be done next.

In Jesus' name,
Amen.

SELF-PUBLISHING

EDITOR

Dear God,

Give me wisdom about who should be the editor for this book, who should beta read, and when I should send it out. Give me wisdom throughout the process and help me take any constructive criticism in a healthy manner. Help me tell the difference between constructive criticism, which will help strengthen the style and heart of the book, and criticism based on a personal preference. Help me listen to my beta readers and editor, but also help me not compromise the heart of the book to please other people. Let me work in harmony with these people. Help me glorify You in this.

In Jesus' name,
Amen.

EDITOR PRAYER ANSWERED

Dear God,

Thank You for my editor! She's helping me figure out many things in this book and how to change them. This is eliminating a lot of stress. Yes, there is a lot to do, and I need to remember to not expect too much of myself each day, as long as I still make progress in the editing process. Thank You again, Lord. Guide us both with wisdom for this work.

In Jesus' name,
Amen.

THE BOOK COVER WITH A DESIGNER

Dear God,

Lead me to a professional designer who would make an excellent cover design for the book, someone who will understand the tone of the book and translate it into great visuals.

Give me the words to say in detailing the tone of the book and my vision for the book cover so the designer knows what to do. Give us both peace in the process.

Help me work well with the designer and trust what he or she has to say about what would look professional while being true to the tone of the book. If a visual concept art for the cover is not right for the book, help me communicate specifically what needs to be different to the designer.

Help me be a reasonable client. Provide whatever I need to pay the designer well.

Let the book cover appeal to the book's audience, and let it bring glory to You through its excellence.

In Jesus' name,
Amen.

THE INTERIOR DESIGN

Dear God,

Help me find a professional typesetter for the book. Like with the cover designer, help us communicate really well with each other and understand what the other person means. Help me explain the tone of the book so the interior designer will know what to do.

Let the font and white space make the book easy to read, let it look professional, and let the aesthetic match the tone of the book really well in the end.

In Jesus' name,
Amen.

PRICE OF THE BOOK

Dear God,

What should the price be for the book I'm selling? Not so much that it's expensive, but enough that it will allow me to make some profit, I suppose. Help me decide and stick to a price. Thank You for helping me figure this out. Help people understand the value of the book. Thank You for Your patience, Lord. It's greater than my own. Shape me so that I am more patient. Let Your will be done in my heart today.

In Jesus' name,
Amen.

FEARS

FEAR OF SUCCESS

Dear God,

I realized that I am afraid of being an author. Afraid of success. Afraid of becoming prideful. Afraid of not being successful. The future is unknown. Help me keep writing anyway, because I know You put in me the desire to write. Give me peace. No matter what happens, no matter whether I get only a few readers or several million, I want to please You, Yahweh, by the continual surrendering of my heart to Your transformation process. As Jesus said, I can do no good thing without You. Thank You for living in me, comforting Holy Spirit.

In Jesus' name,
Amen.

John 15:5

FEAR OF HAVING NO MORE IDEAS

Dear God,

I'm afraid that one day I'll run out of ideas for books. Let me know that everything is going to be okay and that You are pleased with me. I want this outlet so I can worship You in a creative way, Lord. Help me know that You accept me just as I am and that even if I never wrote another book, You would love me just the same. At the same time, let healthy confidence grow inside of me that I won't run out of ideas, but that my creative well will be filled with really good ideas. I give this to You and trust You no matter what happens. Help me live in the present moment now and not worry about the future so that I can enjoy today and bring my best self to it, trusting You to help me.

Thank You, God, for never leaving me alone. Thank You for helping me today. Thank You for Your constant love and Your never-changing truths. Thank You for who You are. Glorify Your name today. Let Your perfect will be done in me today as it is in heaven.

In Jesus' name,
Amen.

Proverbs 3, Psalm 37

FEAR OF TALKING ABOUT THE BOOK

Dear God,

Please tell me how to tell my friends and family about my book. I don't really know how to bring it up or explain what it's about. Give me peace about it.

Help them take it well. Give me favor and help me accept their favor as a gift from You.

Help me have the right perspective in all of this.

Let none of this cause chaos in my group of family and friends. Let it only bring glory to You, God, and bring people together.

In Jesus' name,
Amen.

FEAR OF NEGATIVE REVIEWS

Dear God,

Help me keep my composure no matter what kind of reviews the book gets. If I need to, help me keep myself from reading the reviews. But also, if I do read a bad review, please encourage me and help me get through the emotions that come. Help me laugh it off and not take myself so seriously. Help me remember that my book is valuable, and help me notice and be encouraged by the good reviews for the book. Please let there be good reviews, Lord. Please remind the readers to write reviews for the book. Let them be touched by the book in such a way that they would automatically want to write a good review for it. Also, help me gracefully receive any constructive criticism that's written in the reviews so that I can further improve my writing. Help me not take it personally but use it to strengthen myself as a writer.

In Jesus' name,
Amen.

Psalm 56:3-4

FINDING SUPPORT

SUPPORT GROUP

Dear God,

I really need a support group, Lord, but I'm not sure how to go about finding one. Please help me in the process of finishing and promoting this project, and bring about a support group of devoted fans who will help me get the word out for this project and let it gain traction and find all sorts of people that I could never reach by myself. Let the right people be in this support group, help us be a blessing to each other.

In Jesus' name,
Amen.

WRITING EXCERPTS

Dear God,

Please send help. I know it would be good for me to put together some writing samples in case I need to share my writing with a critique group, mentor, potential boss, client, editor, agent, or other person in the publishing industry, but I don't know what excerpts from my writing to put together. Help me prepare good excerpts that give an idea of what my stories are about. Prepare me for whatever feedback comes. Help me take it courteously.

In Jesus' name,
Amen.

ASKING FOR HELP

Dear God,

Today, I want to begin asking people if they want to read my work and give me feedback on it, but something holds me back. Give me the courage to reach out to people, talk about my story, and ask them if they would like to read my work and give me feedback on it. Give me boldness and humility. Guide me to the right people that I should ask, give me discernment for when to ask them and what kind of feedback I should ask for.

Give them wisdom and discernment in what kind of feedback to give me once they have read it, so that whatever they say is accurate and helpful. Help me identify which feedback they give is good and which feedback I should let go of discreetly. Help me apply the helpful suggestions to my writing.

Let Your will be done in me today, Lord.

In Jesus' name,
Amen.

MARKETING

STRATEGY

Dear God,

Soon, it will be time to start marketing the book. I'll need a strategy. I've got some ideas, but when I calculated it, I realized that I'll need to do more marketing to really get the book out there. Whom should I ask to see if they would be interested getting the news out there? Maybe I'll ask a few bloggers if they would be interested in having me as a guest writer for a blog post about the book. And maybe I'll spend some money on ads.

Please guide me through this process. Help me get the book out there to many people I haven't even met.

Also, help me not overdo any area of marketing but find a balance between online and in-person marketing. Show me what I can do, and help me work with my strengths and limitations.

I'll be getting to work on it soon. Thank You for supporting this book.

In Jesus' name,
Amen.

MARKETING WITH CONSIDERATION

Dear God,

Please help me market this book in a way that is considerate of others. I don't want to just sit back and think the book is going to sell itself, but I also don't want to become that annoying salesperson on the internet who wants everyone to buy their book. Give me guidance about how to be considerate of everyone and market the book in a way that is both appealing to others and true to the tone of the book. Help me bring glory to You in this.

In Jesus' name,
Amen.

ADVERTISING

Dear God,

There is so much I could do when it comes to advertising and marketing. Help me stop thinking about how stressed I'm feeling. Give me discernment about how much time I should work on this and how much of this stuff I should even do. I want to trust You with the numbers, but I know I need to do my part as well so that a good amount of people can find out about the book. Help me have peace about the idea of becoming a public figure as an author, or give me a good pseudonym that will appeal to people so that I can remain a private person.

Ultimately, help me not care so much about what people think of me, God. I know what matters most is what You think about me. And no matter what I do, You love me so much and call me Your beloved.

In Jesus' name,
Amen.

Matthew 6:34

PART III
LIFE

DEAR GOD,

Please, help me experience Your love today.

In Jesus' name,
Amen.

Romans 8:35-39, Ephesians 3:12-21

GOD

COMMITMENT

Dear God,

I believe. I believe that the Word became flesh. I believe that Jesus came to earth, fully human and fully God in an awesome paradox. I believe that Jesus died and fought for my eternal life. I believe that love defeated death, and that Jesus rose from death to life forever. He cannot die anymore.

I want to follow You forever. It may be hard, I know. Still, I will rely wholly on You. Lead me where You will. Do whatever You want in me for the sake of Your goodness. Allow me to have a deeper understanding of all this, because it is a revelation to me. Keep me always in Your arms, Lord. I can trust Your love will never lead me away from You. I am Yours. Thank You.

In Jesus' name,
Amen.

Isaiah 53, Romans 3:19-31

DEVELOPING FAITH

Dear God,

Thank You for everything that led up to the moment I first believed in You and touched eternity, whether or not I felt it in my soul.

Give me wisdom of ways to develop my relationship with You. Lead me throughout my life into goodness and all that You want for me.

Help me develop relationships with the believers You place in my life. Teach me how to simply be with You, and to become more and more like Christ, as well as more and more who You created me to be.

In Jesus' name,
Amen.

HOW TO PRAY

Dear God,

Teach me how to pray. Sometimes I feel like I'm being fake when I pray to You, but then again, words are often so limited to express how I feel.

How do I pray? Sometimes I feel like I'm wearing a mask that I believe is my bare face, and I don't want that to be the case, Lord. I'm afraid of what's underneath all my masks. You say to come as I am. So here I am, Lord, whether or not I'm wearing a mask, whether or not I'm being "correct" in however I pray.

Thank You for accepting me as I am and working with that. You are my Lord, but You also call Yourself my friend. And then again, You are also my heavenly Father. Teach me what all this means — who You are to me, and who I am to You. I don't know what's supposed to happen in a relationship between God and a human, except some kind of patient transformation into the image of Christ. I am Yours. Help me accept whatever transformation You want to work within me this year. Thank You. I am Yours.

In Jesus' name,
Amen.

Matthew 6:6-15

A NEW DAY

Dear God,

Thank You for waking me up this morning and providing food for me. Thank You for giving me breath today. Please, help me experience Your peace today, because You are the prince of peace. Help me carry Your peaceful presence to the people around me. I let go of my worries about tomorrow and the future so that I can focus on bringing glory to You today in how I live and write. Help me become a peaceful person, someone who lives with grace and humility, without worry.

I will give up my unhealthy desire for control because I choose to trust You with my life instead, knowing that You are for me, and every good and perfect gift comes from You, Lord. Help me continue to do this in the future.

In Jesus' name,
Amen.

James 1:17-18

AN URGE TO PRAY

Dear God,

Whenever I get the urge to pray, sometimes something pulls me back and almost makes it sound like it would be dumb to pray about this to You. But it's not dumb at all. Please, help me not think it dumb to pray about anything that matters to me. I believe You care about even the small things. Give me the urge to pray more often. Remind me to take time to stop and listen to You, too. I want to begin taking time to stop and sit in Your presence, listen to Your kind voice, and thank You for everything You have done for me.

Thank You for hearing me and helping me come closer to You, Lord. I'll listen now and expect to hear Your loving voice and recognize it. Even if I don't hear Your voice today, I will expect it and keep coming to You to try to hear You. I choose to expect that You will show up in my life in ways that surprise me.

In Jesus' name,
Amen.

Luke 12:6-7

CLEAR CONSCIENCE

Dear God,

If there is anything in me that offends You or anything wrong I have done that I have not made right, make it known to me and show me how to fix it, whether I need to ask someone for forgiveness or I need to forgive someone. Help me through this process of forgiving others, asking for forgiveness, and receiving your forgiveness if that is what I need to do.

If there is anything I need to change in my life to make things right between You and me, let me know and guide me through the process of restoration. I will rely on You to transform me from the inside out, because You are the only one who can truly correct and heal me.

And lastly, change my heart towards anyone I am holding a grudge against or resenting. Help me see them the way You do and act in genuine love towards them, no matter what I think they deserve, for You have forgiven me of more than I could ever know.

I choose to take a step in the right direction today; lead me into Your genuine goodness.

In Jesus' name,
Amen.

Psalm 103:11-13, Psalms 139, 1 John 1:7-9

FAITH

Dear God,

Please give me faith. Faith that things will work out. Faith that I will get through this. Faith for my family. Faith for my friends. Your Word says that faith is a powerful thing, that it makes things happen. I don't know about all the times when it seems like it's not enough, or when there's more going on underneath the surface, but I want to have faith anyway. Please give me faith. It will help me. Faith is one of the last three things that will remain, and I want to take part in it.

In Jesus' name,
Amen.

1 Corinthians 13

UNDERSTANDING FAITH

Dear God,

Give me a greater understanding of what faith is and what it requires, because I don't know if I understand it well enough. What is the purpose of faith? Do we need faith to live in You? Why does faith please You? Why is it spiritually necessary in Your Word? How do I build up my faith in You?

Thank You for Your wisdom, Lord.

In Jesus' name,
Amen.

Hebrews 11, Luke 17:5-6, John 6:29

SERVANT

Dear God,

I don't want my prayers to merely be me trying to get things from You and not being willing to do what You want me to do. I really do want to serve You. I want to love You as I should and to love people as Jesus does. Please transform me into someone who enjoys being around You and serving You, someone who won't forget You no matter how good or bad my life gets.

I will rely on You. You are working in me even when I don't see it.

In Jesus' name,
Amen.

TRUST IN GOD

Dear God,

You are good. There is no evil in You. Teach me what I need to understand so I can trust You better.

I want to trust You. This is so important for my relationship with You. Let me begin to trust that You are always with me, always caring about me, always working on my behalf. Let me know that even when something goes wrong, it wasn't you who made it happen. Show me that You will always be there to comfort and lead me. You don't judge me, and I can be close to You.

I choose to trust You to save me. I want to trust You to provide for me. I want to trust You to keep me from falling away from You in the future. I want to believe that You will always forgive me no matter what. Help me forgive everyone who has hurt or offended me. Help me trust You to heal me and to heal my family members and friends emotionally, physically, and spiritually, whether it takes a long time or a short time. Help me trust You even when things go wrong. Let me know You care when someone dies or falls ill. Show me how You are trustworthy. Help me see it and believe.

You can and will bring good out of any hard situation. Thank You for hearing me. I choose to believe You will answer me. Let Your will be done on earth as it is in heaven, Lord, for no one is injured, sick, or anxious in heaven.

In Jesus' name,
Amen.

Psalm 126, Hebrews 11

FINDING GOD THROUGH THANKS

Dear God,

I don't want to say thank You right now, because I'm in a bad mood. Help me find something to thank You about, even though I want to say something bad.

Okay. I choose to say thank You. Thank You for being patient with me.

Sometimes I wonder if I'm faking it — if I'm not really thankful to You but am saying it because I know I should be saying it to You. Saying thank You is a sign of faith, I've heard. Saying thank You in faith that You will answer, or have already answered, my prayers. Help me get through today's problems.

All I can do to protect myself from doubting Your goodness right now is to say thank You and count the things I am thankful for. Help me find You. Thank You for Your grace.

In Jesus' name,
Amen.

Psalm 136

CONFUSION

Dear God,

There are so many different opinions about the meaning of several Bible verses, and it all confuses me. I don't know who to believe. I wish there was a standard out there that would help me know if what one preacher said was true or false. Even in the midst of this confusion, I do know that You are loving, compassionate, merciful, faithful, and generous. That will help me some. Teach me true discernment of Your Word, Lord, so that I don't fall astray to just any teaching.

I wish I knew the original languages of the Bible so I could read it in those languages. Even so, without historical context, I might get confused about some scriptures anyway.

Lead me to a good commentary that will help me learn cultural context and the full meaning behind the Greek and Hebrew words. May Your word come alive to me. Give me wisdom. Lead me to truth about You. Strengthen my understanding and faith. Thank You, Lord, for Your faithfulness in my life even when I am confused.

In Jesus' name,
Amen.

James 1:5-8, Hebrews 1

ANGRY AT GOD

Dear God,

I think I'm angry at You for something. Or maybe I just resent You. I wish I wasn't angry at You. I think it's something I sometimes hide. But the thing is, I don't want to be angry at You. But I am. And I don't know what to do about it, God. It's almost like I don't believe You really care about me, because I've gone through so much.

I don't know what to ask for. I just don't want to be angry at You anymore, God. I want to see You the way You are and not from my limited perspective. I want to know that You, Creator, are only good and that You care about me and that I can be close to You and find healing in Your arms. Please, let me see this truth and be able to accept it.

In Jesus' name,
Amen.

OLD WOUNDS

Dear God,

Help me heal from wounds caused by what I used to believe about You or things I used to be taught. I think I still, deep down, have those wrong beliefs about You. Help me see You not as the mean God who only lets in those who are perfect. Allow me to see You as the God who loves everyone and accepts everyone who comes to Him. Help me accept this and trust this is true. Let me know it in my heart, not just in my mind.

Help me know and accept that I can't earn Your love, but I can accept Your gift of love and a better kind of life even though I don't deserve it.

Help me let go of the pride that keeps me from accepting Your grace. Teach me to let go of the doing-to-please mentality that ultimately fails, since I'm not perfect, and allow me to find, accept, and hold on to the mindset that You have. Transform me from the inside out into who You want me to be.

In Jesus' name,
Amen.

Romans 7, 8

LIMITATIONS ON GOD

Dear God,

I want to stop limiting in my mind who You are. You are far bigger and more complex than I can imagine. Show me the ways that I have wrongly been limiting You, and help me quit.

Help me to accept You as You are, God, even when I can't understand You. I want to allow myself to experience the vastness of You, the vastness of Your love, the vastness of Your power, the vastness of Your desire for relationship with me. I want to understand what all of this means for my life.

Let all my revelations of You be aligned with scriptural truth. If there are verses I have interpreted incorrectly, lead me to the truth that helps me see Your goodness in a new way.

I think I have placed limitations on You in my mind because I have been afraid of being disappointed, that You're not involved in our lives after all. It is like I have only been pretending that I believe You are real, and so I have not been living like I actually believe You are real.

Help me change, Lord. Let me not be afraid of experiencing wonder and disappointment. I don't want to let this fear keep me from living full-heartedly anymore. There's an adventure here just waiting to happen if I will just let myself be vulnerable before You.

Open my eyes and help me allow myself to be courageously vulnerable with You, to develop a new sense of wonder for You in every day. Let this vulnerable wonder change the way I live and write in beautiful ways that please You. Let no one harden this, not even myself.

In Jesus' name,
Amen.

THE EMPTINESS ONLY GOD CAN FILL

Dear God,

Please fill the emptiness inside me. Show me how to live in Your love. Please increase my faith, Abba, so that it is enough for me to do what You ask of me.

In Jesus' name,
Amen.

John 14, John 15, Hebrews 13:20-21

COMFORT

Dear God,

I need Your comfort today. Please, hold me close to Your heart. Let me know You are here with me and that You take my tears seriously. Hold me close. Let me feel Your love. Take these burdens and grant me rest.

In Jesus' name,
Amen.

Psalm 56:8

GOD'S MAGNIFICENCE

Dear God,

You are the most powerful being in existence. It's hard to believe that I can talk to You. Usually, people high up are impossible to talk to, but You want to talk with me? That is amazing to me.

You are the most creative being in existence, and You made the moon. You made stars from the command of Your voice.

Wow. I am actually talking to You!

God, You are huge. You are infinite. I can't even imagine infinity.

You are the source of love itself.

When I think about this, I begin to see You differently. I get overwhelmed by how big You are, how powerful You are, how creative You are, and how beautiful You must be.

You are merciful and patient. You are compassionate and active in my life. So many wonderful things in my life came from You that I have not even thought of.

Thank You.

In Jesus' name,
Amen.

THE INFINITENESS OF GOD

Dear God,

Help me embrace Your infiniteness with open arms. Help me not try to understand it, because I am human and limited by the physical world. Protect me from being terrified of the infinite in all its forms — from the idea of heaven being forever to the idea of You having always existed. Help me not hurt my head over it, but lead me to the things You want me to understand. Comfort me and bring me peace. You are my true home.

In Jesus' name,
Amen.

Psalm 131

TO BE MADE HOLY

Dear God,

I read in the Bible that You want to make Your children holy — set apart for a divine purpose. Teach me what this means. Make me holy, then, as You want me to be.

In Jesus' name,
Amen.

Hebrews 12, 1 Thessalonians 5:23-25

ARMOR OF GOD

Dear God,

Help me know what it means to wear "the full armor of God," how to put it on, and how to keep wearing it every day in every situation, metaphorically.

Help me know and build up my faith that You want me to write my book and that I can write it in the amount of time that I have to write it.

Help me strengthen my faith in my identity as Your redeemed child, Abba, for that is the helmet of salvation.

Help me build up my faith in Your goodness, Your faithfulness, and Your truthfulness.

Help me sharpen the sword of the Spirit that You have given me, and help me understand how it works in my life.

Help me understand the belt of truth's importance in my life and wear it well wherever I go.

Help me wear the breastplate of righteousness wherever I go and help me understand what it means to wear it.

Help me carry the shield of faith everywhere I go so that I can use it against the fiery darts of the enemy, Lord.

Help me wear the gospel shoes wherever I go, and help me understand what it means to carry the gospel everywhere I go.

In Jesus' name,
Amen.

Ephesians 6:10-18

BOLDNESS TO CHASE GOD

Dear God,

Help me get rid of everything that keeps me from chasing after You with all that I have. I want to know You far better than I ever have before. I want to be as close to You as possible. I won't care about what the world says. I won't care about what anyone says about my radical faith. I love You, Jesus. I love You, God. You are my loving master, my gentle counselor. You are more gorgeous than I know. Take away everything that makes me think that I need to "play it safe" and not get "too excited" about You, God. You are my passion. You are what my heart longs for, God. Thank You for this boldness, Lord. Lead me from here on a journey to experience and live out of the infiniteness of Your love and Your Holy Spirit for the rest of my life and forever after. I want to follow You and obey You with everything in me. You are worth far more than the whole world.

In Jesus' name,
Amen.

Hebrews 12

HOLY AWE

Dear God,

I'm realizing the gravity of the facts that I am praying to You, that You hear me, and that prayer changes things. I'm in Your holy courts right now, praying to You. Yet, You're also the God of peace, and You give me peace. Thank You for not destroying me for my imperfections. I could weep. I am completely in Your hands. You are so big. Before, I said that You were powerful and huge because I imagined it in my head and knew it from what the Bible says, but now I'm beginning to see the reality of those statements and tremble before You. Yet, You tell me to rest. You provide it for me. You take care of me. I am speechless.

In Jesus' name,
Amen.

Psalm 23, Psalm 27

RAGING LOVE

Dear God,

Your love is a raging fire, constant, never-ending, calling me. You have my attention. Help me allow Your love in more areas of my life. I don't want to push You aside anymore or ignore You. Your love isn't just a liking for me. It's not a small thing. It's intense and longs for my attention.

I'm here.

You understand me far more deeply than anyone else, including myself. How do I come closer? You are beautiful and You long for me even though I am nothing; but You made me. I am one of Your beloved children.

God, I worship You and sit before You, thankful for Your closeness yet longing to be filled more deeply by You.

In Jesus' name,
Amen.

Song of Solomon 8:6-7, Revelation 1:14

татаTO LEARN

Dear God,

Teach me the secrets of creativity, of art, of stories. Reveal to me the hidden rules or possibilities that no one has discovered yet. Show me how to go far beyond mediocrity in this work, fueled by the Holy Spirit inside of me. Let this work challenge and inspire others to seek You in everything they do so that they can bring God-inspired creative solutions into the world and draw people to You through the work of the Holy Spirit. Let Your will be done on earth as it is in heaven, Lord. Let Your name be glorified everywhere.

In Jesus' name,
Amen.

Proverbs 25:2

HOLY SPIRIT

FRUIT OF THE SPIRIT

Dear God,

Develop in me all the fruits of the Spirit as I seek You more and more. I can't live without You, and I can't change myself. Only You can transform me, and I trust You to do that as I meditate on Your scriptures, Your truths, Your love, Jesus' character. I want to be like Jesus. I want to consistently live in love, joy, peace, patience, kindness, goodness, faithfulness, gentleness, and self-control. Shape me in Your image, not my own. Let Your will, which is always good, be done in me today and the rest of my life.

In Jesus' name,
Amen.

1 Peter 2:2-3, Galatians 5

BAPTISM OF THE HOLY SPIRIT

Dear God,

The Bible says You command that I be baptized in the Holy Spirit, not just with water. Show me what that looks like. Baptize me in the Holy Spirit, Lord, so that I see Your power manifest in my life as with the apostle Paul and the early church. I receive the Holy Spirit, as You have commanded. Help me understand what this means for me and what Your will is for me. I choose to trust You in this, though I don't know what will happen. It's outside my comfort zone. But I know You are good. I will trust You.

In Jesus' name,
Amen.

Luke 3:16, John 20:19-22
Acts 1:8, Acts 2, Acts 19:1-7

A LIFESTYLE OF PRAYING IN THE SPIRIT

Dear God,

Remind me to speak/pray in tongues as a lifelong habit because it says in the Bible that doing so helps build up my faith and renews me. Help me continually see the ways that praying in tongues is helpful to me. Help me know when to do it and when not to do it so that I don't disturb other people or make them uncomfortable. Encourage me in this and help me know the validity of my prayer language. Lead me to other people who also pray in tongues and help us bring it up in conversation so that we might encourage each other.

In Jesus' name,
Amen.

1 Corinthians 14

SPIRITUAL GIFTS

Dear God,

Thank You for filling me with Your Spirit. Help me recognize any spiritual gifts You have given me, and develop them within me, Lord. Give me wisdom about Your will for me concerning them. Lead me, and let Your will continually be done within me.

If one of my gifts is encouragement, give me discernment. If I have the gift of strong faith, give me wisdom and discernment regarding what to believe for. If I only have one gift and it happens to be giving words of knowledge, give me discernment for when to speak and when to be silent. If my gift is speaking in unknown languages, or speaking in tongues, lead me in that. If my gift is prophecy, give me wisdom and discernment for when it is true prophecy and when it is simply my own opinion. If my gift is healing, show me how and when to pray for people.

Whatever gift or gifts You have given me, teach me how to use them. Help me be a good steward of them and not forget to use them. Help me do my part in the body of Christ. Protect and keep me from misusing the gifts You have given me. Teach me humility. Create in me a loving heart.

In Jesus' name,
Amen.

1 Corinthians 12

THE UNKNOWN

Dear God,

How much of what I believe is actually true? There is so much I do not know. And there is so much confusion in the world about You that I can begin to doubt everything if I think about it too much.

But I have realized that I will have to be okay with the fact that I will never know everything. To have faith is not to have certainty, but to believe based on some evidence in the face of doubt.

Today, I will choose courage even within the unknown. I may not know the complete truth while I am alive, so I will keep living with faith anyway, trusting in You, my heavenly Father. I will keep seeking wisdom while holding on to what I have learned from the Bible. Above all, I will remember to allow Your love to transform me into someone who loves others generously.

Thank You for being here with me
in the middle of the unknown.

In Jesus' name,
Amen.

1 Corinthians 13

COMMUNICATING ABOUT A HOLY SPIRIT EXPERIENCE

Dear God,

Something so beautiful, amazing, and good has happened in my life, but I don't have the words to explain it, yet. Don't let me dismiss it. I want to remember this in the future. I want to be empowered by what has happened, and I don't want to slip backward into doubt. Help me process and understand what has happened to the degree that You want me to understand it. There are some parts I probably won't ever completely understand on earth or in heaven. But I want to write about this. I feel speechless about it.

When the time is right, Lord, help me to write or speak about what has happened to me in a way that is true and helpful.

Sometimes, when I'm trying to tell someone about a miraculous experience, I fall completely short and try to explain it away out of fear that the person would not believe that it was God who made this wonderful thing happen. Sometimes, I try to act like it was not a huge event that changed my life out of fear of sounding crazy. Help me communicate the story without a mask that downplays it. Give me wisdom about whether I should keep this to myself or share it with others.

And if I should share it with others, show me when to talk about it and who to talk to about it. Give me wisdom about how much to say. Thank You, Lord, for this incredible experience.

In Jesus' name,
Amen.

Isaiah 6

WORSHIP

WORSHIP AS LIFESTYLE

Dear God,

Teach me what true worship is. What does it mean to worship You in spirit and in truth? How should I worship You? Teach me what it means to know You and fellowship with You, and also what it means to sit in Your presence.

Give me wisdom about how to worship You every day, how to be truly reverent towards You and how to do everything in service to You.

Help me turn away from anything that has kept me from You so that I can worship You with a clear conscience.

Consume my entire life with Yourself, Lord. May I think of You when I get up and when I go to bed.

Consume my entire life with Yourself so that when something goes wrong, the first thing I do is pray, and when something goes right, the first thing I do is thank You.

I want to be deeply and profoundly excited to live with You every day of my life, for You are good.

In Jesus' name,
Amen.

James 4:7-8, Psalm 8, Psalm 150

TRUE WORSHIP

Dear God,

Help me worship You even in the midst of this hard situation. It's so hard to have a clear focus on You. I want to be genuine, but it's hard to stay focused. Please help me focus and help me see how beautiful You are and how good and loving You are even now. Help me praise You, God. Help me believe You will come through for me, even if it's in a way I don't expect. But also, help me love You and worship You for who You are and not for what You do for me. Make my heart right. I don't know more than You, God. You know more than everyone in the world combined and multiplied. You are so creative and beautiful. Thank You for drawing me to You. Thank You for saving me and having a relationship with me. Thank You, God, for who You are. I will listen to Your beautiful voice today and expect to hear it.

In Jesus' name,
Amen.

Psalm 42, Habakkuk

ENOUGH

Dear God,

I have been overwhelmed with the knowledge that nothing I do in my own power will ever be enough to adequately worship You. I have fallen to my knees, in awe of Your glory. Am I enough? I am dirt. And You made that, too. Yet You made me to know You, to worship You, and to experience Your love and share it with people.

Perhaps my incompleteness is enough. Maybe You don't require worship that expresses the fullness of Your being — only a heart that is willing to bow to You and know that You accept it.

You accept my incompleteness and offer infinite love in return.

I accept it. I pray this infinite love fills me up to overflowing and heals me and lives in me and guides me every day of my life and forever.

I worship You in my incompleteness paired with Your infinity within me. Maybe it's enough now. I'm enough with Christ inside of me.

Thank You, God, for this mystery.

In Jesus' name,
Amen.

IN GOD'S PRESENCE

Dear God,

Now that I'm here with You, I don't even want anything. I feel Your presence, and it is enough. I know You're always with me, but today I'm more aware of this truth, and it produces this peace within me. This space is sacred, and I am still. Thank You. I think I'll sit in silence with You for a while.

In Jesus' name,
Amen.

Psalm 16

HEALTH

HEALING

Dear God,

Heal me, physically, emotionally, and spiritually. Let me live a long life, happily doing what You meant for me to do. Use the state I'm currently in for Your glory. Protect me from harm. Heal my soul. And my mind. Help me be willing to get whatever help I need, whether it be from a doctor, a counselor, a pastor, or all three. Bring good solutions into my life that will bring true and permanent healing to my body. Provide the way for me to become healthier physically, and give me willingness to care for myself. Help me become more disciplined in doing the things I should be doing to improve myself. My body is Your temple, after all. Let Your will be done in my heart so that I can take care of myself better.

Take care of me, Lord, even when I don't know how to take care of myself. Thank You for loving me like a good father loves his children.

In Jesus' name,
Amen.

Proverbs 19:8, Psalm 103

SELF-IMAGE AND FLAWS

Dear God,

Help me be okay with the way I look, not being disgusted by myself or judging myself for not taking care of myself as well as I could. To some extent, I can't help how I look. You made me, so I need to accept that.

You're perfect and beautiful. Let me not be ashamed of my body, Lord. Let me not be ashamed of my face or my hair or anything else. Instead, help me see what You see. Let me see what's beautiful about my physical features and be content. Even more importantly, let me see what's beautiful about my heart.

I'm going to learn how to accept myself as I am. This includes: my body, my emotions, my likes, dislikes, my abilities, strengths, and my flaws, whether they be perceived flaws or real ones that need to be worked on. That's important to You, because You accept me as I am. I know I can improve, and I will, but it's important that I accept myself first, allowing Your grace to flow over me and to work in me.

Help me with this, Lord. Help me embrace this process with patience.

In Jesus' name,
Amen.

Psalm 139

THANKFULNESS

Dear God,

Thank You for my personality and my heart. Thank You for giving me the desire to write books. You care about the books I want to write. You care about excellence and the heart of each book. You are the most creative being. You are the most beautiful being.

In Jesus' name,
Amen.

LONELINESS

Dear God,

I don't want to feel lonely like this. I know You made humans to have relationships with each other. Lead me to the right kinds of people and help me find the right people to befriend. If there are friends I haven't talked to in a long time, guide me to talk with the right ones. Give me wisdom about how to communicate with them.

Make it possible for me to talk to people regularly as I should, but also help me spend time with You. Show me how You fill the big hole in my heart with all of You. Tell me what I need to do in my life to fix this empty feeling if there is anything else missing. Help me glorify You better for having this loneliness and sadness filled up with Your fellowship and then sharing Your love with people, and with the satisfaction of doing good work. If there are any medical causes for this lonely and sad feeling, whether it be a vitamin deficiency, lack of sleep, or something else, let me know and help me find the things that will really make it better. Thank You, Lord, for hearing and answering me and taking care of me.

In Jesus' name,
Amen.

Psalm 25:16, Psalm 27:10, Psalm 56:8, Psalm 68:5-6, Matthew 12:18, Isaiah 46:3- 4, Matthew 28:20, Romans 8:31-38

DELIVERANCE FROM A TOXIC SITUATION OR ENVIRONMENT

Dear God,

Deliver me from all evil.

Deliver me from this toxic environment,
or strengthen me with Your truth
and life till I can leave.

Deliver me from despair.

Deliver me from hopelessness.

Deliver me from temptation.

Deliver me from evil.

Deliver me from wrong influences.

Remove all toxicity if there is any inside me.

Draw me into the truth.

Draw me into the truth.

Draw me into the truth.

Capture my heart, Jesus, and put me where
You want me to be. Show me what to do.

Use me for Your glory, Jesus.

Fill me with Your light and love.

Transform my life.

I want to live for You and not for myself.

In Jesus' name,
Amen.

JOURNALING

Dear God,

Show me how to journal in such a way that
helps me see Your hand at work in my life.

Help me find the time to journal regularly
or however often I need to journal.

In my daily entries, help me always find one
positive thing to write about after a negative thing.

Teach me to value my life story enough
to do it justice with words, even if
I'm writing it down just for me.

If I'm not ready to process a certain experience yet,
help me set it aside till I am ready to write about it.

Protect my journal from prying eyes.

Help me respect this journaling practice
and, if it is necessary for my mental health,
acknowledge it as a need. Heal me in this
process, Lord, even from things I didn't realize
needed healing. Let Your will be done in me.

In Jesus' name,
Amen.

THINKING CLEARLY

Dear God,

I've been worrying way too much. If I sat down and tried to figure out just how much time each day I've spent worrying about this issue, it would be a long time. Show me what I should be focusing on each day instead of that.

Teach me how to think. Help me begin to rewire my mind, ask myself the right questions, and remind myself of Your truths to stop me from worrying. I don't want to worry anymore.

Teach me how to focus on what is true, what is beautiful, what is good, and what is eternal. Show me how to healthily cope with everything that is going on. Show me who You want me to be and shape me into that person.

In Jesus' name,
Amen.

Philippians 4

EXTREMES

Dear God,

I realized that I struggle with thinking in extremes, having extreme fears that don't even make sense, or trying to block out any possibility of an imperfection of mine so as to avoid feeling shame. Help me see both negative information and positive information side by side in a healthy balance so that I can think more clearly and take care of myself better.

Help me see the good things about myself next to my flaws while accepting myself where I am right now, knowing that no one is perfect. Help me see the good in someone I dislike, so that I can see that person more clearly, even if I need to distance myself from them.

Help me overcome the extreme, irrational fears that I've struggled with, Lord, so that I can be a healthy individual.

Let Your wonderful will be done in my life, Lord. Everything good comes from You.

In Jesus' name,
Amen.

SLEEP

Dear God,

Please let me sleep really well tonight. Let me have good dreams. and let me slowly get to bed at a more decent time so that it is easier for me to get up early. Help me not have anxiety or depression or hopelessness tonight.

There is always hope.

You are always with me. Angels are protecting me. Help me not be stressed about anything that happened or was said today, or anything that's going on soon. I give all of this to You, Lord. You will take care of me. You're my dad. Sing me a song tonight, or help me think about a story idea, or guide me to what to think about as I drift off to sleep. Teach me how to manage my mind with grace and ease. I give You all my burdens. I receive Your peace and vision. Thank You for who You are, Lord.

In Jesus' name,
Amen.

Psalm 4, Psalm 91

KINDS OF REST

Dear God,

Give me wisdom about different kinds of rest. Rest from work, rest from writing, rest from reading, sleep at night, rest in Your presence, resting in who You are, everything. I want to know how to take care of myself better so that I can live a better-quality life. Shape my life, Lord, so that every part of it pleases You.

In Jesus' name,
Amen.

Psalm 127:1-2, Matthew 11:28-30, Hebrews 4:1-3

A REVELATION

Dear God,

I have realized something, like the breath of revelation. The truth that Christ lives inside me and that You are working inside me makes me beautiful.

Thank You, Abba, for Your grace, mercy, and patience.

In Jesus' name,
Amen.

RELATIONSHIPS

A FRIEND

Dear God,

Please bring a special friend into my life who can push me to write. Someone who appreciates me and loves me unconditionally. Someone who, without me asking them to, regularly tells me to write and work on whatever I'm working on. Someone who can encourage me and read my work and appreciate it while also being able to tell me what needs work. If it's not too much to ask, could You bring this person within close proximity to where I live? I pray that this friendship lasts forever. Show me how I can be a blessing in this friend's life as well. Show me how to be an excellent listener, too. Show me how to love this person, how to cause them to feel loved, and how to allow them the safe space they need to become who You made them to be.

Help us both be good friends to each other, showing each other Your love for us and praying for each other whenever we need it. Help us stay connected to each other over the years. Let Your will be done in this.

In Jesus' name,
Amen.

Proverbs 18:24

RELATIONSHIPS

Dear God,

Please help me form and maintain healthy relationships with the right people. Let me be in the right place at the right time. Form within me the right kind of heart for every relationship You bring into my life so that I genuinely love people. Help me accept people as they are and not try to control or change them, and help me be attracted to emotionally healthy individuals who will not abuse my compassion for them. Let me attract friendships with people who accept me as I am, people who are safe for me to talk to about deep things. Help me open up to trustworthy people, Yahweh. Help me find my accountability people.

Let me recognize the people You have placed in my life for a purpose and appreciate them wholeheartedly, Lord. At the same time, prevent me from worshiping any human or relying on anyone in unhealthy ways.

Show me how to have a healthy, satisfying relationship with You where I am, giving up what I should give up and receiving what You have for me, knowing that You are a God of healthy relationships and that You are perfectly loving.

Help me treat everyone with the kind of love that comes from You, God, so that when people see me, they see You.

Show me how to be a better listener to the people around me, God. Thank You for transforming me into the image of Christ.

In Jesus' name,
Amen.

Proverbs 13:20, Proverbs 18:19, Psalm 146

PRIDE

Dear God,

I don't want to define myself in terms of "better than" or "worse than" others. We're all the same because we're all imperfect. Lord, keep me from indulging in any form of self-worship because everything I have comes from You. Every talent is something You gave me, and I can't take them for granted nor say that I "earned" them. Another thing: I don't want to define myself every day by whether I have enough of something or whether I have done enough good deeds or whether people approve of me and my decisions. I don't want my self-worth to come from knowing a lot or "having a lot of wisdom" or having gone through a lot of bad stuff.

God, teach me how to let myself be small — and not so I'm "better" than people who aren't humble. Lord, I don't know how to be free of this pride.

It's not like I'm better than anyone else. God, help me. I've realized that this pride has been keeping me from receiving Your love, and it has kept me from showing compassion to myself. All my life I thought I had to be perfect to be accepted. Even when I was told I didn't have to be perfect, I didn't believe it. Maybe I tried to, but deep down, I know I didn't feel like it was true. Even when I read essays about grace and was enlightened in it and shared my new knowledge with people, I still didn't apply grace to my own life. I didn't know how.

I can't take credit for the good things I do, because they came from You. You also gave me the desire and faith I needed to be saved. Help me accept this. It makes me small.

In Jesus' name,
Amen.

John 15:1-5, Galatians 6

TO BE A BETTER FRIEND

Dear Lord,

Teach me how to be a better friend. I feel like I haven't been the best friend I could be. I don't know what step to take next. Teach me to love the way I should love people. Show me the right way to value myself. Show me how to see the world. Shape me.

In Jesus' name,
Amen.

John 13:12-15

REACTIONS

Dear God,

So many people that I know are going through hardships of all sorts, and I don't know how to react to them. Show me how much I should educate myself about different hardships and help me be a good listener to whoever needs me to listen.

Help me be able to provide comfort to at least some of the people in my life, Lord. I know there's only so much I can do without either exhausting myself or crossing a line of interfering in other people's business; teach me where that line is, Lord. Give me wisdom about where I can help, where I can be a good listener, and where I can bring encouragement that is helpful and not hurtful or annoying to whoever needs it. If there's something I can do to help, give me wisdom and divine ideas, Lord. Use me to show a glimpse of Your love to those who are hurting.

And if I need to take care of myself first, show me how to do that, Lord.

In Jesus' name,
Amen.

Galatians 6:2

HEALTHY BOUNDARIES

Dear God,

I have people in my life who want to spend time with me when I have a lot of writing to do. Help me figure out a good time to set for writing. Help my friends and family members accept this and respect my writing time. Help me actually get writing done during the time period that I've decided to write. Help me be considerate to the people in my life, too, and let our times together be meaningful and enjoyable. Help me break unhealthy habits. In their place, help me form and stick to healthy life habits, focusing on good things and what I have to do instead of negative things. Help me set my own realistic standards for myself instead of lowering them or raising them to the standards of other people. Lord, let me understand Your will in this, and let Your will be done in my life.

In Jesus' name,
Amen.

ENVY

Dear God,

I realized I've been struggling with envy and comparison. I wish I had things that other people have, or that my personality was different, or that my life was normal, or that I could do the things that other people do so easily.

Help me accept where I am right now.

Help me be content with what I have and what I have accomplished.

Take away this envy and keep me from comparing myself to others, or comparing my abilities to other people's abilities, or comparing what I have to what other people have. I choose to believe that I can change, that I can stop envying others with Your help, that I can stop focusing on what other people are doing, and that I can focus on doing what I love with You, Lord.

Thank You, God, for hearing me and helping me change. I want to have faith in You and Your opinion of me, not what others may think of me. Thank You for where I am right now. Thank You for the gifts You have given me. Thank You for the tasks You have given me to do. I value them.

You provide all that I need, Lord,
and I don't lack anything.

In Jesus' name,
Amen.

1 Corinthians 10:13, Proverbs 14:30,
James 3:14-16, Philippians 2:3
Galatians 5:14-15, Galatians 6:4-5, Hebrews 10:36

CHURCH HOME

Dear God,

Help me find a really, really good church home for me where I know my purpose and feel like I belong. Give me courage to actually go there and talk to people afterward. Help me find people who can connect with me the way I need to connect with people right now where I am at. Let someone talk to me who ends up becoming a good friend and anchor at the church. If I need to ask for prayer for something, please give me the courage to do so and explain it in an understandable but tactful way.

Help me find the people I need in my life, God, and help us accept each other. If I need a spiritual mentor, please bring one into my life, and make it possible for us to meet and talk; put together appointments for us to meet and talk.

You do care about me, Lord. Thank You for everything You do; You are always good.

In Jesus' name,
Amen.

Hebrews 10:23-25

UNITY IN THE CHURCH

Dear God,

You long for unity in Your Church throughout the world. Please unify us in the Holy Spirit. Work inside of us however You want, Lord, and bring peace, love, and unity within the Church despite the intricate differences among us all that sometimes cause discord. Give us a greater understanding of what kind of unity You want in the Church.

Lord, work inside of me. Help me do my part, however big or small, in bringing unity in the Church. Give me wisdom about my behavior, and lead me away from pride and into humility. Help me love Your Church better, Lord. Give me wisdom about what it means for me to love Your Church the way I should, Lord.

In Jesus' name,
Amen.

John 17

DRIVING

Dear God,

Whenever I drive, teach me to be considerate of others. Teach me to not stay angry at traffic or speeders. Transform me into someone who is quick to dismiss any negative thoughts when someone does something annoying or offensive. Help me give the benefit of the doubt to strangers. You are so forgiving and patient with us, Lord. Help me show grace too. Help me pay attention and do my part to keep everyone safe. Keep me safe on the roads, Lord. Thank You.

In Jesus' name,
Amen.

UNBELIEVER

Dear God,

Someone I know doesn't believe in You. Please lead him back to Your love and help him know You are truly good. If there's anything more I can do, let me know, but if it's not my place to talk to him, let me know that, too. Please send other people into his life who can challenge the way he is thinking in a better way than I can; let them point him in the right direction. Break his heart in the best way, Lord, and help him come back to You and find healing and satisfaction for his soul. Help me love him the way You love him, and if there is anything in me that is not of You, Lord, replace it with Your goodness. Let Your perfect will be done.

In Jesus' name,
Amen.

OFFENSE

Dear God,

Teach me not to be troubled or offended so easily when people disagree with me or treat me a certain way. Help me not react in anger or annoyance to whatever is said or done. I know it's not good to listen only with the intention of replying with my own opinion. Help me stop doing that. Instead, help me relax, be civil, be kind, and listen so I can understand their side. Help me to stop dehumanizing people who are different than me. Let me stop being afraid of people who are different than me and help me see them as valuable. Show me how I can change in this area, Lord, taking steps in the right direction, so that I can be a part of the process of Your Church becoming unified. Let Your perfect will be done in my heart and life.

In Jesus' name,
Amen.

FAMILY

Dear God,

I don't really know how to love my family better. I don't know how to respect my parents better. They mean well. I don't know how to love my siblings better. Teach me how to understand them better and know what I can do to communicate to them that I appreciate them. Change my heart for the better, Lord. Let Your perfect will be done in me. Thank You for my family.

In Jesus' name,
Amen.

HUMILITY

Dear God,

Teach me humility. Help me humble myself and see myself as neither worse nor better than everyone else. Let me see myself as human, and remind me how You see me, Lord. Show me how to be honest with myself and with You. Show me who I am. Help me accept my limitations. Help me know how small I am in the grand scheme of things and how powerful and big You are. Reveal to me Your healing love and show me that knowing You is enough. Help me be willing to write for the amount of people that You want me to write for, Lord. Shape me today. Thank You for loving me and for making me Yours forever.

In Jesus' name,
Amen.

MATURITY

Dear God,

I've grown so much this past year. Of course, there's so much more I have to learn, but I want to stop and say thank You. Thank You for helping me grow closer to You, Lord. Thank You for helping me grow stronger. Thank You for how far I've come. I'm more confident in You than I was a year ago. I'm healthier emotionally, though I still sometimes struggle. I can't see all the areas where I've grown mature this last year, but You know them, Lord.

Help me be content with where I am now while I continue to learn how to live in You and allow You to live in me. Thank You for Your love. I couldn't have gotten here without You; You have helped me more than I know.

Continue to teach and correct me so that I can live well, fully loved, and genuinely loving others like Jesus loves.

In Jesus' name,
Amen.

WORK & STEWARDSHIP

A GOOD-PAYING JOB

Dear God,

Please provide a secondary job for me that allows me to write at the pace I want to write and still make enough money to live. Allow me to not be exhausted. Let it be a job that is satisfying for me to do on the side and not too stressful, and let the boss/manager be competent, smart, and kind. Help me learn a lot from this job and be the right person for it. Let me bring glory to You at this job. Give me wisdom and peace about where to apply. Teach me how to have a good attitude at my job; I know I'd rather be writing, but I want to appreciate my other job too and look at it as another way to worship You and be a light. Shape me as You will.

In Jesus' name,
Amen.

EDITOR

Dear God,

Lead me to the clients I should work with and teach us both how to work together in harmony. Give us patience, enthusiasm, sound minds, and common sense when it comes to the editing I will be doing. Help me develop an ability for detecting the big pictures of what the authors are trying to accomplish with their works, and help me help authors transform their works into masterpieces while also staying true to the writers' styles. Thank You for this opportunity, Lord. Shape us in this process so that we both improve in our skills, both creative and communicative, and draw us closer to You.

In Jesus' name,
Amen.

VOCATION

Dear God,

Please reveal to me what my vocation could be — what my strengths are, and what I can do with them in the world. Place me where I can be a light doing whatever I am to do, whether it be a particular type of writer, artist, something else, or multiple things with balance. Help me value this vocation and find fulfillment in the work, Lord.

Lead me through each season of my life, and help me see and accept the good that You have for me in each one. Place me among people of integrity, diligence, and faith. Continue to teach me how to value myself the way You value me.

Above all, no matter what I do with my life, I want to be like Jesus.

Help me live and love like Jesus.

In Jesus' name,
Amen.

FOR CARE OF THE EARTH

Dear God,

You are all-powerful, and You care about the state of the earth.

Help me see what is happening and learn what the earth needs.

Please give me understanding of the most important thing I can do to help improve the earth's environment. What causes should I support?

I rely on You. I also ask that You provide wisdom and understanding to the people who have the most power either to improve or harm the earth. Put a passion in their hearts to do what they can to help make and keep the earth a stable, healthier, cleaner place. Help them be ethical and accurate in their methods. Let their efforts be effective and enough.

Let Your will be done for the earth as it is in heaven.

In Jesus' name,
Amen.

SAVING MONEY

Dear God,

I'm often tempted to buy new books or spend the money that I get from my paycheck in unnecessary ways. Teach me to save my money so that I can please You with the ways that I use it. This money is all Yours because You gave it to me. If there's a place where I can invest my money wisely, lead me to that and help me understand how this all works. Let me only put my money where it will glorify You, Lord. Also, I want to begin budgeting. Please help me build a budget that will also help me better appreciate having spending money to buy books. Teach me how to use and save money in ways that glorify You.

In Jesus' name,
Amen.

TITHING

Dear God,

Give me wisdom about how much, how often, and where to tithe. This is important to You, and I want to give what I can give with generosity, willingness, and joy. It's also important that I'm giving it to a Christ-centered church that will be using it for Your glory. Guide me where to give this tithe. Let this not become a thing that I do just because I should do it, but let it become another way for me to worship You, knowing that You provide all my needs. You are amazing, Lord. Thank You for giving me opportunities to give back to You what You have given to me.

In Jesus' name,
Amen.

DEAR GOD,

Humble writers to tell good stories. As they write, draw them to the arms of Jesus.

In Jesus' name,
Amen.

FOR A FAVORITE AUTHOR

Dear God,

I pray for my favorite author, that You would allow him to keep writing amazing books and publish them and that You would make him more successful in this endeavor. Give him revelations about his writing that will allow him to write the best books he's ever written, books that are captivating and meaningful. Let them be well-written. Keep him and his family safe and healthy, and draw them closer to You. If there is anything keeping him from being able to write, or from being able to write the story that You want him to write, help him get through it, Lord, and come alongside him. Let him know he doesn't need to write the story by himself, but that You want to help him write it, too. Heal all brokenness in his life and home. Draw him close to You and bring his books to completion in Your perfect timing. Grant him the favor, wisdom, and humility he needs to overcome the pitfalls of success. Let him bring glory to You in everything he does, and let everything he does prosper.

In Jesus' name,
Amen.

FAMILY MEMBERS WHO WRITE

Dear God,

Help my family members who are writers to be at peace and figure out what they need to figure out so they can write the best books they can write, books that are not only enjoyable but meaningful and captivating. Give them divine inspiration, ability, and desire to finish the books You have invited them to write. Give them hope and emotional healing. If something is keeping them from writing, or from writing as well as they want to, Lord, please let there be a breakthrough. Provide whatever they need, be it confidence or motivation or something else. Keep them safe and healthy and help them begin to see themselves as You see them.

Help me be considerate of their writing time and help me understand how to support them in their writing endeavors.

When it comes time to market the book, Lord, give them wisdom and boldness to do whatever they need to do to get their books out there.

Help us learn to love each other the way You love us. Help us glorify You with this.

Let Your will be done in their lives
on earth as it is in heaven.

In Jesus' name,
Amen.

FOR A FRIEND WHO WRITES (FEMALE)

Dear God,

My friend, _____, is a writer and I really want You to help her with her project. Help me support her and pray for her. Give me wisdom for what to pray for, and let Your will be done in her life as it is in heaven. Let her book become so beautiful and meaningful and satisfying to her and to her readers that it is life-changing in a positive way. Help her also know whether this book is for her alone or for other people as well. Give her peace and confidence, and let her know You love her so much. Help her get her writing schedule down and help her enjoy the writing process. Help her draw closer to You because of this book. Let her glorify You with everything she does, and let everything she does prosper. Satisfy her soul. Keep her safe and healthy. Help her family become unified in Your love. Mend any and all brokenness in her heart. Set Your love and security as a firm foundation within her so that she knows that wherever she is, she is home because You are there with her.

Give her persistence and passion enough to see the book through to its completion. Let the book be finished and shared with the world if it should be, Lord. Give her whatever she needs to complete it and come alongside her, letting her know she is not alone. Help her write truthfully and vulnerably. Breathe life into her characters, world, story, and writing style. Finally, let her and the book have the favor they need, and bring the book into the hands of everyone who would enjoy it. Let it bring glory to You, Lord, and may Your perfect will be done in this.

In Jesus' name,
Amen.

FOR A FRIEND WHO WRITES (MALE)

Dear God,

My friend, _____, is a writer and I really want You to help him with his project. Show me how to support and pray for him. Let Your will be done in his life as it is in heaven. Please guide him in the book he is writing. Give him wisdom about whether it is just for him or for others, too. Let him write this book with You, God, letting You inspire him and give him the endurance he needs. Let it become a deeply meaningful and satisfying journey, and let the end result also be life-changing. Help him write the book as well as it can be written. Teach him what he needs to learn in this process, and let this book change him for the better, too. Remind him to take care of himself while he writes this book, and help those who are closest to him know how best to support him. Let him see the truth clearly and write the book that needs to exist.

Give him persistence and passion enough to see the book through to its completion. Set Your love as a foundation in his heart so that he knows just how much You love him and that he is always home because You are always with him. Satisfy his soul. Heal all brokenness in his life. Let the book be finished and shared with the world if it should be, Lord. Give him whatever he needs to complete it and come alongside him, letting him know he is not alone. Help him write truthfully and vulnerably. Breathe life into his characters, world, story, and writing style. Finally, let him and the book have the favor they need, and bring the book into the hands of everyone who would enjoy it. Let it bring glory to You, Lord, and may Your perfect will be done in this.

In Jesus' name,
Amen.

PRAYERS FOR FRIENDS AND THEIR FAMILIES

Dear God,

Heal my writing friends and their families, physically, mentally, and spiritually. Unify their families in Your love. Draw them close to You. Intervene in their lives wherever there is a sense of powerlessness. Help my writing friends' families support them in their writing and be able to provide what they need while they are writing the books You want them to write, Father.

Wherever there is a mindset of lack, I want You to replace it with the understanding, faith, and expectancy that You will provide for all their needs.

Wherever there is sleep deprivation and/or nightmares, I want You to replace them with peaceful sleep and the knowledge that You keep Your children safe and love them deeply.

Wherever there is resentment and unforgiveness, Lord, bring reconciliation, healing, and the willingness to forgive each other and try to love each other again.

Wherever there is brokenness, Lord, bring healing and restoration through healthy changes in perspective and breaking down the lies. Bring faith back into every heart. Intervene in the lives of my writing friends and their families, Lord, and help them see Your hand in their lives.

Wherever there are walls up against Your love, break them down so that my friends can meet with You and experience beautiful fellowship with You.

Wherever there is hopelessness, bring hope.

Wherever there is helplessness, help them know the power You have made available to them and that there is something they can do.

Wherever there is chaos, bring order and self-control by way of the Holy Spirit.

Wherever there is cynicism and looking at things the way the world sees things, bring a healthy change in perspective, Abba, and help my writing friends and their families see things the way You see them.

Wherever there is loss of identity, let there be a deep and profound revelation of being Your children, Yahweh.

Wherever there is pride, bring humility, honesty, and vulnerability.

Wherever there is resentment against
You, bring reconciliation.

Wherever there is unnecessary hurt and
suffering, help them find a healthy way through
it so that they don't have to suffer anymore.

Wherever there is purposelessness, bring purpose.

Wherever there is a loss of wonder, fill them up
with a new sense of wonder, inspiration, and hope.

Wherever there is loss of innocence,
bring redemption.

Wherever there is weariness, bring
refreshment and new life, new energy,
a new element of Your love.

Wherever there is something not of You, take
it away and replace it with something far more
beautiful that is of You, God of compassion.

Wherever there is unbelief, break
through and let new faith be born.

Wherever someone is not doing what they are
supposed to be doing, redirect their path so
that they can bring more glory to You, Lord.

Wherever there is stinginess, Lord, bring
in a heart of healthy generosity.

Wherever someone is silent who should
speak up, give them a surprising and sudden
boldness to say what needs to be said.

Wherever someone should not be speaking, quiet
them and gently redirect them to the truth.

Wherever there are unhealthy boundaries,
let there be healthy boundaries.

Wherever there is depression, let there be a new
joy that becomes contagious and never goes away.

Help us build each other up with
truth and encouragement.

Teach us how to treat each other in
the midst of disagreements.

Draw all who are lost back to Your arms, God.

Use me as You will in the lives of my writing
friends. Teach me how to love them better.
Teach me how to be a healthier person, with
healthy boundaries. Let us lead fulfilling and
satisfying lives that please You. Help us have
the kind of relationship with You that You so
desperately want us to have. Help us love each
other in the way You so desperately want.

Thank You, Lord.

In Jesus' name,
Amen.

ALL WRITERS WHO ARE CHRISTIANS

Dear God,

Please help Christian writers begin to delve deeper into their relationships with You in a genuine way, finding substance and truth. Let them begin to or continue to have a strong desire to write excellently, and let this desire not go away. Help them discover the steps to true excellence in whatever they are writing and help them write whatever they write out of a genuine heart.

Redirect the writers who should not be published, Lord, and lead them to someplace far more satisfying and good, to their true purpose. Help the writers who shouldn't be published know that the story they are writing is only for themselves and that this is still a beautiful thing.

Redirect the writers who are writing destructive stories and help them see what is true.

Help all of us realize how faulty it is to idolize fame and fortune and help us re-examine our reasons for writing. Help us discover why You want us to write, or what You want us to do instead.

Let us know You, Lord, and be who we are supposed to be.

Use us, and use what we write
for good in the world.

Help us discover and experience Your love
every day and be filled with Your presence.
Satisfy our souls. Help us carry Your presence
into the world, Lord, and bring healing to
everyone we meet. Help us be like Jesus.

Let us hear Your voice, God, and like Jesus said,
let us do even greater things and see amazing
miracles happen in the lives of those around us.

Baptize us in the Holy Spirit like John the
Baptist said Jesus would, Lord. Let Your will
be done in our hearts, minds, souls, and lives.
Help us guard our hearts and understand
what that means to You, Lord. Unify Your
church and teach us to love like You love.

Mend all brokenness. Bring solutions into
our lives and help us accept and use them
and not go back into the brokenness. Help
us walk away from the brokenness forever.
Help us resist temptation to go back to it.

Strengthen our faith. Heal all mental illnesses.

Break all generational curses and all
other bondage that threatens to keep
us from serving You effectively.

Humble us. We choose to trust You. Draw us to Yourself and keep us on the path that leads to You.

Lord of Mercy, let our relationships with You be healthy, genuine, and fruitful. Remove from us everything that is not of You and put within us all that You want to develop within us.

Protect us and keep us safe.

Enrich our works and surprise us with Your goodness. Help us see Your hand at work in our lives, God of forgiveness, and take away all bitterness. Help us worship You wherever we are and with everything we do. Thank You, God! Let Your will be done on earth as it is in heaven.

In Jesus' name,
Amen.

PLACES OF FELLOWSHIP

Dear God,

I ask for multiple places all over the world where Christian writers can meet, fellowship, and find emotional healing. I pray for the places that already exist, that they will be more and more enriched with a sense of comradery. Let no dissension or bitterness dry up these fellowships or break them apart. Let peace find its way there and rule in everyone's lives. Draw Your children close to Your arms, Lord. Let there be paid professional counselors who are very helpful there for anyone who needs a counselor. Let there be gardens. Let there be a chapel. Let there be a place for people to cook. Let there be healing. Let there be safety. Let there be peace. Let there be integrity and divine wisdom in each of the staff members. Let there be healthy community, not merely an echo chamber of similar opinions, nor a place of cliques where people judge each other, but a place of openness where people are encouraged to open up about both grief and joy. Let it not be a place where people are merely acknowledging grief, hurt, and joy, though. Let it be a place of true, permanent, positive transformation in the lives of everyone who comes. Let people have incredible experiences there that they will never forget for the rest of their lives, and let it positively transform their homes and lifestyles upon their return. Help them understand how to use what You have provided them with to change their lives.

Satisfy everyone with authentic experiences of Your love. Let everyone recognize Your hand at work in their lives and know how much You love them. Teach them, then, how to love You and bring glory to You.

In Jesus' name,
Amen.

A PRAYER FOR THE READERS OF THIS BOOK

Dear God,

I pray for whoever is reading these words right now. Give them a genuine experience of Your great, deep, infinite love. Let them not dismiss it. Let it be something they remember for the rest of their lives. Help them love You in return and surrender everything to You in the healthiest way.

Give them a desire for wisdom, a desire to know You more, a desire to serve You without strings attached, a desire and willingness to undergo the process of You transforming them into the image of Christ from the inside out. Reveal Jesus to them, and help them believe in him and rely on him, You, and the Holy Spirit.

Help them develop healthy thought habits and keep them. Restore their souls. Show them who they are in Christ. Help them slow down as much as they need to go on this journey. Help them focus on You and on the Scriptures.

Protect them from evil, and teach them how to engage in spiritual warfare and how to protect themselves when backlash comes on their journey of positive transformation.

Lord, bring good and perfect things
into their lives. Help them find, attract,
and enjoy beautiful things daily.

Heal them continually; lead them on the road
to emotional, spiritual, and physical healing
wherever they may need it. Bring healing
into the lives of their friends and family. Help
them partake in it, Lord. Help them align
themselves fully with You and with Your truths.

Help the ones who are reading this know that
You are so very good, trustworthy, faithful,
just, gentle, loving, strong, patient, fierce, wise,
generous, merciful, unchanging, and firm.

If life is hard for whomever is reading this right
now, Lord, help them. Comfort them. Help them
through this difficult place. Bring people into
their lives to pour love into them and support
them in the deepest ways that they need.

Wherever the reader needs wisdom and
correction, Lord, bring loving and gentle
wisdom and correction as they can receive
it or as they can begin to receive it.

Continue to work within the reader, leading them
back to Your arms forever and ever. Allow them to
become active in this relationship as well, drawing
close to You and discovering how to draw closer
to You. Help them find healing in Your arms, Lord.

Equip them to do wonderful things, big
or small, that will make the world a better
place and point others back to You.

Help them discover, develop, and use
the skills and gifts You place inside of
them, Lord. Help them understand the
purpose for each gift in their lives.

Let Your will be done in them as it is in heaven.

Teach them the nature of Your will so that
they won't be misguided by false voices. Help
them hear Your loving voice in alignment with
Scripture. Help them sense Your guidance.

Help them live well in You, with You,
for You, relying on You, and obeying
You out of a deep love for You.

Deliver them from evil, from the lies, from the
fears they struggle with on a heart level. Guide
them through this process into a life of wholeness.

Let nothing keep them from doing the things
You have for them to do. Bring peace into their
hearts. Complete Your work in them, Yahweh. Let
them know You well and find fullness of joy in
Your presence. Help them love themselves and
the people in their lives the way You love them.

Bless their writing journey. Let it become a way for them to discover You over and over again.

Lead them through life to eventually come home into Your arms.

In Jesus' name,
Amen.

NOTES

ACKNOWLEDGMENTS

When writing a book, many people contribute to its existence without knowing it. Many if not all writers need community and supportive friendships when writing a book for publication.

But before I thank the people who helped this book happen, I want to thank God for keeping me alive and safe this whole time. Lord, thank You for guiding me and being with me. Thank You for supplying the time, energy, and resources I needed to write and publish this book. Thank You for bringing supportive people into my life to encourage me and pray for me during the process.

Nicholas Triplett from Team Greece, thank you for being there in one of the hardest moments of my life. Your help and encouragement have emboldened me to take my purpose seriously.

Thank you to the rest of my Team Greece for your incredible understanding, love, and support. I especially want to thank Chelsea West, Chuck Leupen, and Destinee Dreyer. May God lead you all to good places.

Thank you, Ginger Gregory, for being my official editor!

I want to thank my sister, Lisa Kleefeld, for designing the book cover and interior design for this book and for telling me to finish it when doubts came. Also, thank you for doing a much needed final round of edits with me! The book would not be what it is without you.

Desireé Chorely, thank you for keeping me company over the summers and telling me multiple times that I'd figure the book out when I voiced my frustrations and doubts.

Thank you to the One Year Adventure Novel (OYAN) writing community for your prayers, feedback, support, and ideas for the prayer book. There are so many oyaners I would like to thank personally. Here are just a few of them (ordered by last name or username): Chelsea Beason, Jessica Crespino, Harply, Nattilie Kirby, Hannah McManus, Sarah Beth Meigs, and Garrett Robinson. I also want to thank Mr. and Mrs. Schwabauer for their support.

Thank you to everyone at Oral Roberts University who prayed for or supported me during the process!

Lastly, thank you, my readers, for reading this book!

Happy writing!

CONNECT WITH THE AUTHOR

If you'd like to stay updated on my future books, you can follow my blog at **courtneykleefeld.wordpress.com** and find me on Goodreads, Instagram, and Facebook.

Here are some ways to support this book if you want:

- Tell a friend about it
- Suggest it to your writing communities
- Rate and review it on Amazon and Goodreads
- Make a book review (blog post, social media, video)
- Pin the book cover on a book board on Pinterest
- Buy a copy as a gift for another Christian writer

ABOUT THE AUTHOR

Courtney Kleefeld is an author and musician from Tulsa, Oklahoma. At the time of the publication of this book, she is a fourth-year student at Oral Roberts University, working towards a bachelor's degree in creative writing. In her spare time, she enjoys learning about various mediums of art, reading books, analyzing her favorite stories, and sometimes trying out a new musical instrument for fun. She currently plays piano, harp, and flute, and plans to release music albums with her original songs.

Made in the USA
Columbia, SC
03 July 2025